MTLE

Middle Level Social Studies Practice Questions

Mometrix
TEST PREPARATION

DEAR FUTURE EXAM SUCCESS STORY

First of all, **THANK YOU** for purchasing Mometrix study materials!

Second, congratulations! You are one of the few determined test-takers who are committed to doing whatever it takes to excel on your exam. **You have come to the right place.** We developed these practice tests with one goal in mind: to deliver you the best possible approximation of the questions you will see on test day.

Standardized testing is one of the biggest obstacles on your road to success, which only increases the importance of doing well in the high-pressure, high-stakes environment of test day. Your results on this test could have a significant impact on your future, and these practice tests will give you the repetitions you need to build your familiarity and confidence with the test content and format to help you achieve your full potential on test day.

Your success is our success

We would love to hear from you! If you would like to share the story of your exam success or if you have any questions or comments in regard to our products, please contact us at **800-673-8175** or **support@mometrix.com**.

Thanks again for your business and we wish you continued success!

Sincerely,
The Mometrix Test Preparation Team

Printed in the United States of America

TABLE OF CONTENTS

PRACTICE TEST #1 ___ 1
ANSWER KEY AND EXPLANATIONS FOR TEST #1 ___ 15
PRACTICE TEST #2 ___ 28
ANSWER KEY AND EXPLANATIONS FOR TEST #2 ___ 42

Practice Test #1

1. Which of these pre-Columbian civilizations was Mesoamerican rather than Andean?

a. Inca
b. Aztec
c. Moche
d. Cañaris

2. Of the following European diseases that decimated the Inca population, which epidemic occurred the chronologically latest?

a. Typhus
b. Smallpox
c. Measles
d. Diphtheria

3. Which of the following statements is NOT true regarding the colony of Jamestown?

a. The colony of Jamestown was established by the Virginia Company of London in 1607.
b. The colony of Jamestown became the first permanent English colony in North America.
c. The majority of early settlers died of starvation, disease, or Native American attacks.
d. John Smith's governance helped Jamestown more than John Rolfe's tobacco discovery.

4. Which of the following is NOT a correct statement regarding the Pilgrims?

a. The Pilgrims left England in 1620 on the ship known as the *Mayflower* and landed at Cape Cod.
b. The Pilgrims were led by William Bradford with a charter from the London Company.
c. The Pilgrims were a group of Puritans who left England to escape religious persecution.
d. The Pilgrims were a group of separatists who migrated to leave the Church of England.

5. Which of the following statements is true regarding New Spain in the 1500s?

a. New Spain had not yet developed any kind of class system.
b. The Spanish originally imported Africans to use as slaves for labor.
c. The *hacienda* system eventually gave way to the *encomienda* system.
d. Conquistadores experienced shortages of labor in the New World.

6. Of the following, who was NOT a dispatch rider notifying Americans of British troop movements reported by American surveillance in 1775?

a. Paul Revere
b. William Dawes
c. John Parker
d. Samuel Prescott

7. Which of the following British generals came to Boston in May of 1775 to push General Thomas Gage to become more aggressive toward the American colonists?

a. William Howe
b. Henry Clinton
c. John Burgoyne
d. All of the above

8. Which of the following is NOT true with respect to the Constitutional Convention of 1787?

a. The delegates to the Convention had a common opinion that people are inherently selfish.
b. Convention delegate Benjamin Franklin was quite instrumental in the Great Compromise.
c. Edmund Randolph designed the "Virginia Plan," which was introduced by James Madison.
d. Paterson's New Jersey Plan favoring smaller states was an alternative to the Virginia Plan.

9. Which of the following is NOT correct about the growth of America in the first half of the 19th century?

a. By 1840, two thirds of all Americans resided west of the Allegheny Mountains.
b. The population of America doubled every 25 years during this time period.
c. The trend of westward expansion increased as more people migrated west.
d. Immigration to America from other countries was not substantial prior to 1820.

10. Which of the following was the first canal built in New York State?

a. The Cayuga-Seneca Canal
b. The Chambly Canal
c. The Oswego Canal
d. The Erie Canal

11. Which of the following is NOT correct concerning the growth of American labor unions?

a. The new factory system separated workers from owners, which tended to depersonalize workplaces.
b. The goal of attaining an 8-hour work day stimulated growth in labor organizing in the early 1800s.
c. An early strike occurred in Paterson, New Jersey, in 1828, when child laborers walked off the job.
d. Recurring downturns in the economy tended to limit workers' demands for rights until the 1850s.

12. Which of the following was an example of violence in cities that occurred as a result of rapid urbanization in America in the 1830s?

a. Democrats opposed Whigs in New York City so strenuously that the state militia was called in.
b. Both New York City and Philadelphia experienced a series of racial riots during the mid-1830s.
c. A Catholic convent was attacked and plundered by a violent mob in New York City in 1834.
d. All of the above occurred in American cities during the 1830s.

13. When was the first American transcontinental railroad finished?

a. 1862
b. 1890
c. 1869
d. 1865

14. Which of the following helped prepare the US for entry into World War I?

a. The National Defense Act
b. The Navy Act
c. The Revenue Act
d. All of the above

15. Of the following demonstrations of Soviet disagreements with the US after World War II, which was the first to transpire?

a. The Soviet Union backed Communist control of Hungary and Romania.
b. The Soviet Union endorsed Communist control of Czechoslovakia.
c. The Soviets did not allow conservatives to serve in the Communist government imposed on Poland.
d. Soviets refused to take part in the international Baruch Plan because they mistrusted American motives.

16. Which of the following most accurately describes the group that invaded the Bay of Pigs in 1961?

a. Members of the US CIA
b. A group of Cuban exiles
c. The people of Cuba
d. CIA-sponsored Cuban exiles

17. During the Civil Rights era of the 1950s, which of the following events furthered the civil rights cause?

a. The Supreme Court's decision in *Brown v. Board of Education of Topeka*
b. Governor Orval Faubus' actions relative to Little Rock High School
c. Eisenhower's use of the 101st Airborne Division to protect students
d. Both A and C

18. In LBJ's Great Society program, which of the following was NOT included?

a. Medicare
b. Voting rights
c. Federal aid to education
d. Ending the Vietnam War

19. Which of the following statements is NOT true regarding the events of September 11, 2001, in the US?

a. Shortly after that date the US defeated the Taliban and captured Al-Qaeda leader Osama bin Laden.
b. On September 11, 2001, Muslim terrorists flew two hijacked airplanes into the World Trade Center in New York.
c. On September 11, 2001, Muslim terrorists flew a hijacked passenger airliner into the Pentagon in Arlington, Virginia.
d. An airplane hijacked by Muslim terrorists crashed in Pennsylvania after passengers resisted the terrorists.

20. Of the following, which statement about the US economy in the 1990s is correct?

a. By the year 2000, the US economy was increasing at a rate of 5% a year.
b. The rate of unemployment in America at this time dropped to 6%.
c. The rates of productivity and of inflation in the US were about the same.
d. The US stock market's total value had doubled in only six years.

21. In 20th-century America, which of the following occurred first?

a. The Emergency Quota Act was passed by Congress.
b. European immigration peaked at almost 1.3 million.
c. Congress passed a very restrictive Immigration Act.
d. The Great Depression caused decreased immigration.

22. Of the following events, which had an impact or was associated with the "New Left" of protesting youth in the 1960s?

a. The organization of the Students for a Democratic Society (SDS)
b. The organization of the Berkeley Free Speech Movement at UC
c. The assassinations of Martin Luther King, Jr. and Bobby Kennedy
d. All of the above.

23. Which of the following rivers did NOT play an important role in the development of the earliest civilizations?

a. The Tiber River
b. The Yangtze River
c. The Euphrates River
d. The Nile River

24. The Indus Valley or Harappan civilization existed in all of the following modern countries EXCEPT:

a. Iran
b. India
c. Pakistan
d. Turkey

25. The Yellow River Valley began to emerge as a cultural center during the:

a. Shang Dynasty
b. Neolithic Era
c. Xia Dynasty
d. Paleolithic Era

26. Which of the following choices is NOT true about early Christian monasticism?

a. At first, all monks were hermits modeled on St. Anthony the Great.
b. Pachomius organized his followers into the first monastery in 318.
c. Basil the Great in the West, and Benedict in the East, were leaders.
d. The rule of St. Benedict was the most common of medieval rules.

27. The Renaissance which began in Italy subsequently spread to which of the following other countries in Europe?

a. England
b. France
c. Germany
d. All of these

28. Which of the following played the most influential role in the Spanish defeat of the Incas in the 16th century?

a. The scarcity of roads in the Incan Empire prevented the Incas from easily defending their cities.
b. Francisco Pizarro's forces outnumbered the Incan warriors.
c. The centralized power structure of the Incan Empire left the Incas vulnerable after Atahualpa was captured.
d. New diseases introduced by the Spanish decimated the Incan army.

29. Which of the following is a correct statement regarding consequences of the French Revolution?

a. De Tocqueville wrote that it showed the rising middle class's growing self-awareness.
b. Conservative Edmund Burke felt it was a minority conspiracy with no valid claims.
c. Marxists viewed it as a huge class struggle with lower and middle classes revolting.
d. All of these statements are correct regarding consequences of the French Revolution.

30. Which of these is NOT true relative to the rise of Fascism in Europe?

a. Fascism was opposed to nationalism and to patriotism.
b. Fascism was opposed to Marxism and the bourgeoisie.
c. Fascism purported to be an alternative to Bolshevism.
d. Fascism had some things in common with Bolshevism.

31. Decolonization was difficult or impossible in countries with large, long-term settler populations where the settler population was too important and/or the indigenous population had become a minority. Of the following countries, which one had a settler population that moved out and relocated upon the country's decolonization?

a. The Chinese population of Singapore
b. The large Jewish population of Algeria
c. The British population of Cayman Islands
d. The Russian population of Kazakhstan

32. Of the following statements, which was NOT a characteristic of the Nuclear Age in the 1950s?

a. The 1950s were a decade of nuclear optimism, as nuclear power was seen in a positive light.
b. While almost everything was expected to become atomic, cars were not yet included.
c. People expected that the atomic bomb would replace all other earlier kinds of explosives.
d. Nuclear power was expected to replace all other energy sources such as coal or oil.

33. Which of the following statements is false regarding the Puritans?

a. In terms of their theology, the Puritans were considered Calvinists.
b. Many Puritans agreed with radical views that criticized the Swiss Calvinists.
c. Many of those identified as Calvinists opposed the Puritans.
d. The Restoration and the Uniformity Act reunified the Puritan movement and the Church of England.

34. Which of the following statements is *not* true of the rash of witch hunts that took place in the 14th through 16th centuries in Europe?

a. The witch hunts used the Inquisition's techniques for rooting out heretics.
b. Many hunts followed careful legal codes.
c. Much of the evidence used was based on hearsay.
d. Belief in magic and superstition was commonplace even among educated Europeans.

35. Which factor of the Neolithic Revolution most directly contributed to the practice of trade?

a. More freedom for people to choose where they lived
b. The rise of new religious practices
c. The ability of communities to stockpile surplus food
d. New advances in tools

36. Who did NOT write about the concept of the Social Contract, which was incorporated into the Declaration of Independence?

a. Thomas Hobbes
b. John Locke
c. Jean-Jacques Rousseau
d. Benjamin Franklin

37. Some American colonists reacted angrily to Great Britain's Navigation Acts in the seventeenth and eighteenth centuries primarily because of which of the following?

a. The Acts restricted manufacturing in the colonies.
b. The Acts forced the colonists to buy sugar from the French West Indies.
c. The Acts gave the British a monopoly on tobacco.
d. The Acts placed high taxes on the cost of shipping goods to Britain.

38. "This era represents the golden age of the Roman Empire. For about 200 years, the Empire experienced relatively few attacks, stability among its conquered lands, and significant developments in architecture and the engineering of roads and bridges. This time period saw the greatest expansion of the empire and the Romanization of the western world."

The above passage refers to which era of Roman history?

a. The reign of Julio-Claudian line of emperors
b. The reign of the Five Good Emperors
c. Pax Romana
d. The reign of the Flavian Emperors

39. Who were the Angles and Saxons?

a. Viking invaders of England.
b. Groups from French Normandy.
c. Members of the emerging middle class.
d. Two of the many Germanic groups who competed for dominance after the fall of Rome.

40. Under feudalism, this term refers to a person who controlled a large landholding and gave parts of it away in exchange for loyalty and protection.

a. Fief.
b. Homage.
c. Lord.
d. Primogeniture.

41. Civic responsibility differs from personal responsibility in that the subject matter of civic responsibility is mainly which of the following?

a. Fair reporting of government actions
b. Fair dealings between governments
c. A person's responsibilities as a citizen
d. A person's responsibilities as a government worker

42. Which court case established the Court's ability to overturn laws that violated the Constitution?

a. *Miranda v. Arizona*
b. *Marbury v. Madison*
c. *United States v. Curtiss-Wright Export Corporation*
d. *Brown v. Board of Education of Topeka*

43. What are the first ten amendments to the Constitution more commonly known as?

a. The Civil Rights Act
b. Common law
c. The Equal Protection clause
d. The Bill of Rights

44. What percentage of votes does the Senate need to pass a bill?

a. Two-thirds majority
b. A simple majority
c. A supermajority
d. Three-quarters majority

45. The concept of due process in the Fifth Amendment to the U.S. Constitution protects individuals in which of the following ways?

a. Guaranteeing a citizen's right to a trial by jury within a reasonable timeframe
b. Restricting the government's ability to remove basic rights without following the law
c. Guaranteeing a citizen's right to equal protection under the law
d. Restricting the government's ability to remove basic rights without dire cause

46. The Animal and Plant Health Inspection Service, the Food and Nutrition Service, and the Forest Service are members of which department?

a. The Department of Health and Human Services
b. The Department of Agriculture
c. The Department of the Interior
d. The Department of Transportation

47. A filibuster is used to delay a bill. Where can a filibuster take place?

a. The House of Representatives
b. The Senate
c. Committees
d. The Supreme Court

48. Which organization is maintained by Congress to oversee the effectiveness of government spending?

a. The House Committee on Oversight and Government Reform
b. The Office of Management and Budget
c. Government Accountability Office
d. The Department of the Interior

49. Disagreements between individuals or organizations are tried in:

a. Civil court
b. Criminal court
c. Federal court
d. State court

50. What best describes the way Washington, D.C. is governed?

a. Congress has ultimate authority.
b. Washington, D.C. has a local government similar to that of other cities in the area.
c. There is no local government in place.
d. There is a mayor and city council, but Congress has the authority to overrule their decisions.

51. How many Southern states originally ratified the 14th Amendment?

a. Three
b. Five
c. One
d. Ten

52. To be President of the United States, one must meet these three requirements:

a. The President must be college educated, at least 30 years old, and a natural citizen.
b. The President must be a natural citizen, have lived in the US for 14 years, and have a college education.
c. The President must be a natural citizen, be at least 35 years old, and have lived in the US for 14 years.
d. The President must be at least 30 years old, be a natural citizen, and have lived in the US for 14 years.

53. The president may serve a maximum of _____ according to the ___ Amendment.

a. Three four-year terms; 23rd
b. Two four-year terms; 22nd
c. One four-year term; 22nd
d. Two four-year terms; 23rd

54. What effect do minor political parties have on the elections?

a. They are too small to threaten major parties.
b. They take funding away from major parties.
c. They often work with the major parties.
d. They can potentially take votes away from major parties.

55. People are typically made aware of political culture, facts, and values through family, friends, society, and:

a. Media
b. Census takers
c. History
d. Gun ownership

56. Which Supreme Court case enforced the civil rights of citizens to not incriminate themselves?

a. Marbury v. Madison
b. Miranda v. Arizona
c. Youngstown Sheet and Tube Company v. Sawyer
d. United States v. Carolene Products Company

57. Most state governments have a bicameral legislature. Which one of the following states does not?

a. Utah
b. Nebraska
c. Washington
d. Louisiana

58. Which of the following landmasses is *not* part of the Ring of Fire?

a. Japan
b. Cascade Mountains in Washington
c. Andes Mountains in South America
d. Mount Kilimanjaro

59. On a map of Africa, there is a small box around Nairobi. This city is depicted in greater detail in a box at the bottom of the map. What is the name for this box at the bottom of the map?

a. Inset
b. Legend
c. Compass rose
d. Key

60. The shortest distance between New York and Paris goes:

a. Over Florida and Spain
b. Along the 42nd parallel
c. Near Labrador and Greenland
d. Over Philadelphia and London

61. Which of the following nations is NOT a member of OPEC?

a. Saudi Arabia
b. Venezuela
c. Yemen
d. Iraq

62. Antarctica will appear the largest on a

a. Mercator projection
b. Robinson projection
c. Homolosine projection
d. Azimuthal projection

63. Where is the area of greatest corn production?

a. South Africa
b. Kazakhstan
c. United States
d. Mexico

64. In the plate movement known as ____, an oceanic plate slides underneath a continental plate.

a. faulting
b. spreading
c. subduction
d. converging

65. What is the name for a brief interval of coolness in between warm periods in the Pacific Ocean?

a. La Niña
b. Tropical gyre
c. El Niño
d. ENSO

66. Which best reflects the consensus among early childhood experts regarding sleeping routines for young children?

a. Parents should be in young children's bedrooms nightly until they fall asleep.
b. Parents should not be in young children's bedrooms to allow self-soothing.
c. Any family choice should be consistent for promoting good sleeping habits.
d. Family beds for parents and children are currently preferred by US experts.

67. What is the name for the traditionally Arab district in a North African city?

a. Souk
b. Medina
c. Wadi
d. Bazaar

68. The rocks and landmasses that make up the earth's surface are called the

a. atmosphere
b. biosphere
c. hydrosphere
d. lithosphere

69. In the United States, what is the correct term for a settlement with fewer than 100 inhabitants?

a. Village
b. Town
c. Hamlet
d. City

70. Which type of chart is best at representing the cycle of demographic transition?

a. Pie chart
b. Political map
c. Line graph
d. Flow-line map

71. On a political map of India, the northernmost part of the border with Pakistan is represented as a dotted line. Why is this so?

a. Pakistan does not have control of this border.
b. This area has never been comprehensively mapped.
c. Indian Sikhs are threatening to secede.
d. The borders of the Kashmir region remain in dispute.

72. Which of the following is *not* one of the Baltic states?

a. Moldova
b. Latvia
c. Lithuania
d. Estonia

73. Thai food has become increasingly popular in the United States, though it is prepared in slightly different ways here. This is an example of:

a. Cultural divergence
b. Assimilation
c. Cultural convergence
d. Acculturation

74. Land is typically more expensive in urban areas than in rural areas. Which geography concept does this reflect?

a. Location
b. Distance
c. Pattern
d. Interaction

75. Which of the following would NOT happen if the FOMC uses Treasury Bills to pursue a contractionary monetary policy?

a. The money supply decreases
b. The international value of the American dollar increases
c. The price of US goods to foreigners increases
d. Lower interest rates

76. How is the long-run Phillips curve different than the short-run Phillips curve?

a. In the long-run Phillips curve, there is a trade-off between unemployment and inflation.
b. In the long-run Phillips curve, unemployment is always greater than inflation.
c. In the long-run Phillips curve, there is no trade-off between unemployment and inflation.
d. In the long-run Phillips curve, unemployment equals inflation.

77. Which of the following is NOT true of monopolistic competition?

a. There are no great barriers to entry or exit from the market.
b. Firms within monopolistic competition benefit from product differentiation.
c. Firms within monopolistic competition maximize profit by producing where MR = MC.
d. Firms in monopolistic competition are efficient.

78. Which of the market structures is most efficient?

a. Perfect competition
b. Monopolistic competition
c. Oligopoly
d. Monopoly

79. In the long run, firms will exit a monopolistically competitive market when:

a. Profit is maximized
b. Price = marginal cost
c. Price exceeds marginal cost
d. Price is less than the minimum of the average total costs curve

80. In economic terms, which of the following is considered investment?

a. Buying a new home computer
b. Construction of a new manufacturing plant
c. Purchase of a college education
d. Selling finished goods to a customer

81. What must nominal GDP be multiplied by to arrive at real GDP?

a. GNP
b. Price Deflator
c. Supply
d. Demand

82. Which of the following statements about the long run aggregate supply (LRAS) curve is correct?

a. The horizontal part represents high levels of unemployment.
b. The curved part represents high levels of unemployment.
c. The vertical part represents high levels of unemployment.
d. The LRAS curve is a straight, vertical line.

83. Assume the Fed acts to try to keep rising prices stable. Which theory suggests that unemployment will increase as a result?

a. Phillips curve
b. Business cycle
c. Circular flow model
d. Classical economics

84. Which of the following would NOT cause aggregate supply (AS) to change?

a. An increase or decrease in land availability
b. The labor force suddenly increases dramatically
c. A new oil discovery causes dramatic decreases in power production
d. Worker productivity remains the same

85. The government increases spending by $1,000,000 and the multiplier is 5. How does this affect aggregate demand (AD)?

a. It has no effect.
b. AD will increase by $5,000,000.
c. AD will increase by $200,000.
d. AD will decrease by $5,000,000.

86. Which of the following statements is NOT true?

a. If the government imposes a tax on a good, the supply curve will shift to the left.
b. If the government imposes a tax on a good, it will result in a deadweight loss.
c. If the government imposes a tax on a good with a highly inelastic demand, it will be difficult for producers of the good to shift the cost to consumers.
d. If the government imposes a tax on a good, the market price of the good will likely increase.

87. How does unionized labor in an industry typically affect the wages of workers in that industry during a downturn in the economy when AD decreases?

a. It makes wages more likely to decrease
b. It makes wages more "sticky"
c. It has no effect on wages; instead, it causes AS to decrease
d. It has no effect on wages; instead, it causes AS to increase
e. It makes wages more likely to increase

88. The value of a "market basket" of goods and services in one year compared to the value of the same goods and services in another year is known as what?

a. CPI
b. GDP
c. GNP
d. CCI

89. A business takes out a one-year loan to pay for an investment on January 1. On December 31 of that year they pay the loan back. During that time, the nation experiences a recession, and the overall price level in the economy drops. Which of the following statements is true?

a. The nominal interest rate of the loan is greater than the real interest rate.
b. The real interest rate of the loan is greater than the nominal interest rate.
c. The nominal interest rate of the loan is greater than the nominal rate.
d. The loan has a real interest rate but not a nominal rate.

90. The value of the goods and services exported by a country within a year and the goods and services imported by that same country during the same year is captured most directly in what?

a. Balance of payments
b. Current account
c. Capital account
d. Financial account

Answer Key and Explanations for Test #1

1. B: The Aztec was a Mesoamerican civilization of the pre-Columbian period. The Aztecs were ethnic groups of central Mexico dominant in large areas of Mesoamerica in the 14th-16th centuries. The Inca (A) was an Andean civilization from Peru. The Incas had the largest pre-Columbian empire, including Peru and major parts of Argentina, Bolivia, Chile, Colombia, and Ecuador in the 15th and 16th centuries. The Moche (C) was an Andean civilization in northern Peru between 100 and 800; this civilization is known for their artworks, architecture, and irrigation systems. They built the Huaca del Sol, an adobe pyramid that was the largest pre-Columbian construction in Peru before the Conquistadores destroyed part of it. The Cañaris (D) was an Andean tribe living in the south central part of Ecuador. The Incas eventually conquered the Cañaris, but the Cañaris resisted this conquest for many years. They were also known for their architecture, which had many Incan influences. They existed until their main city, Tumebamba, was destroyed by Atahualpa during the Inca Civil War in the 16th century.

2. C: Measles was the latest epidemic listed to attack the Incas, in 1618. The earliest was smallpox (B), which killed half the Taíno population of Hispaniola (now Haiti and the Dominican Republic) in 1518 and virtually wiped out the Aztecs in Tenochtitlan (now Mexico City) by 1521. Smallpox killed an estimated 60-90% of the Incas by the 1520s, with repeated epidemics in 1558 and 1589. An epidemic of typhus (A) in 1546 caused more deaths among the Incas. The 1558 smallpox epidemic was accompanied by an epidemic of influenza, killing even more Incas. An epidemic of diphtheria (D) added to the death toll in 1614. The measles epidemic of 1618 (C) attacked the remnants of the Inca culture. European colonizers unwittingly imported these diseases. Since the Europeans had developed antibodies to the infections through many years of exposure, it never occurred to them that the Native Americans had no such exposure and hence no immunity. This lack of immune defenses made the diseases much more virulent to the Indians than they had ever been to the Europeans who carried them. As a result, a majority of Native Americans died from diseases introduced by Europeans.

3. D: It is not true that John Smith's governance helped Jamestown more than John Rolfe's discovery that a certain type of East Indian tobacco could be grown in Virginia. Smith's strong leadership from 1608-1609 gave great support to the struggling colony. However, when Smith's return to England left Jamestown without this support, the future of the colony was again in question. In 1612, however, when John Rolfe found that an East Indian tobacco strain popular in Europe could be farmed in Virginia, the discovery gave Jamestown and Virginia a lucrative crop. Therefore, both Smith's time in office and Rolfe's discovery were beneficial to Jamestown. Jamestown was established by the Virginia Company of London in 1607, and it became the first permanent settlement by the English in North America. It is also true that Jamestown survived in spite of the fact that most of its early settlers died from starvation, disease, and native attacks. It is also true that many of Jamestown's settlers came from the English upper class and were unwilling to farm the land, while others came hoping to find gold or other treasures, and persisted in their search for these instead of working to make the land sustainable.

4. C: The Pilgrims were not Puritans seeking to escape religious persecution in England. They were actually English Separatists (D) who believed there was no fixing the Church of England, and thus chose to separate from it. They did embark on the *Mayflower* in 1620, and storms drove the ship to land at Cape Cod, Massachusetts (A). Their leader was William Bradford, and they had been given a charter by the London Company to settle America (B) south of the Hudson River.

5. D: The conquistadores had to deal with labor shortages during their colonization of America in the 16th century. To address the shortage of labor, the Spanish first used Indian slaves. Only after the Indians were decimated by diseases brought from Europe and from being overworked did the Spanish begin to import slaves from Africa (B). The first system used by the Spanish was the *encomienda* system of large estates or manors, which was only later succeeded by the *hacienda* system (C), which was similar but not as harsh. It is not true that New Spain's society had no kind of class system (A). In fact, this society was rigidly divided into three strata. The highest class was Spanish natives (*peninsulares*), the middle class consisted of those born in America to Spanish parents (*creoles*), and the lowest class was made up of Mestizos, or Indians.

6. C: Paul Revere and William Dawes were both dispatch riders who set out on horseback from Massachusetts to spread news of British troop movements across the American countryside around the beginning of the War of Independence. John Parker was the captain of the Minutemen militia, who were waiting for the British at Lexington, Massachusetts. Samuel Prescott, a young physician, joined Paul Revere and William Dawes along their route.

7. D: General William Howe (A), General Henry Clinton (B), and General John Burgoyne (C) were all British generals who came to Boston in May of 1775 to push General Gage to pursue further aggression against Americans.

8. C: James Madison was the one who designed the Virginia Plan. Edmund Randolph, a more proficient public speaker, introduced this plan at Madison's request—not the other way around. It is true that the Convention delegates believed that humans are basically selfish by nature (A), which was why they instituted checks and balances in the constitution to keep the government or any part of it from abusing its powers or acquiring too much power. Benjamin Franklin was instrumental in the Great Compromise (B), which was reached with his help after the convention went into deadlock over choosing the Virginia Plan or the New Jersey Plan. The New Jersey Plan, designed by William Paterson, was offered as an alternative to the Virginia Plan (D), as it would give smaller states equal influence as larger states. The Great Compromise incorporated elements of both plans by having the equal representation outlined in the New Jersey Plan in the Senate and the representation based on population outlined in the Virginia Plan in the House of Representatives.

9. A: By 1840, more than one third of all Americans lived west of the Alleghenies, but not two thirds. It is correct that in the first half of the 19th century, the American population doubled every 25 years. It is also correct that westward expansion increased as more people moved west during these years. It is correct that there was not a lot of immigration to the US from other countries before 1820. It is also true that foreign immigration to America increased quickly around that time, with most immigrants coming from the British Isles.

10. D: The Erie Canal was officially opened on October 26, 1825, and connected the Hudson River to Lake Erie. The Cayuga-Seneca Canal (A), connecting the Erie Canal to Cayuga Lake and Seneca Lake, was first used in 1828. The Chambly Canal (B) is a Canadian canal in Quebec that was opened in 1843. It is not a part of the New York State Canal System, as the other canals listed here are. The Oswego Canal (C), which connects the Erie Canal to Lake Ontario at Oswego, was opened in 1828. In 1992, the New York State Barge Canal was renamed the New York State Canal System, which incorporates all of the canals listed in this question except for the Chambly Canal (B), which is not in New York State.

11. B: Option b is not correct. In the early 1800s, labor organizers were aiming to reduce the workday to 10 hours, not 8 hours; the 8-hour workday was not widely realized until 1938–1940. The other options are accurate. The new factory system separated workers from owners, which depersonalized workplaces, and child laborers conducted an early organized strike in Paterson, New Jersey in 1828. While this strike was one of the earliest by child workers, it was not the very first American labor strike — that distinction goes to a 1751 protest by bakers who stopped baking bread. Recurring economic downturns in the 1800s also limited the frequency and effectiveness of labor organizing, keeping workers more dependent on employers and less likely to take action.

12. D: All of these are examples of urban violence in 1830s America. Political differences between Democrats and Whigs in New York City escalated into such violent fighting that the state militia was called in to subdue the disagreeing parties (A). Race riots broke out in New York City and Philadelphia during this decade (B). An angry mob in New York even went so far as to raid a Catholic convent in 1834 (C). All of these events were attributable to the very rapid influx of people to the cities, causing mob violence and street crime to grow out of control.

13. C: The first transcontinental railroad was finished in 1869 (C) on May 10. Construction on the railroad was begun in 1862 (A) but not completed until seven years later. After completion, economic depression prevented more railroad building until the 1890s (B). In 1865 (D), there were 35 000 miles of railroad track in the country; by 1890 (B), there were 200 000 miles. The first transcontinental railroad connected the Central Pacific Railroad, which began in Sacramento, California, to the Union Pacific Railroad, which began in Omaha, Nebraska, in Utah.

14. D: All of these laws prepared the US for entry into World War I. The National Defense Act of 1916 (A) expanded America's armed forces, and the Navy Act (B), also in 1916, expanded the US Navy. In that same year, the Revenue Act (C) created new taxes to finance the growth of America's military.

15. C: The earliest instance of Soviet-US differences was in 1945 when the USSR establishment of a communist government in Poland, which prohibited conservative participation (C). In 1947, the Soviets backed the Communist control of Hungary and Romania (A). In 1948, the Soviets also supported communist rule in Czechoslovakia (B). Later the USSR refused to participate in the Baruch Plan (D), which aimed to set up an international agency to manage the use of atomic energy. This action demonstrated an unwillingness to cooperate with other nations in the interest of peace. These events signified the beginning of the Cold War.

16. D: The 1961 Bay of Pigs invaders would best be described as Cuban exiles sponsored by the CIA. It was not members of the CIA themselves (A). It was a group of Cuban exiles (B), but this answer is not as correct as choice D, which further specifies that these Cuban exiles were sponsored by the CIA. They were also trained by the CIA and supported by US armed forces. The people of Cuba (C) did not invade nor did they support the invasion. In fact, the invasion was quashed by Cuban armed forces within three days.

17. D: Both answer A and answer C furthered the civil rights cause, but answer B impeded this cause. In the case of *Brown v. Board of Education of Topeka*, the Supreme Court's 1954 ruling stated that schools segregated by race are by nature not equal. This ruling was monumental in the NAACP's fight against school segregation. Orval Faubus, Governor of Arkansas, tried to prevent Little Rock High School's integration in 1957 (B). The situation escalated to the point that President Eisenhower nationalized the Arkansas National Guard and sent the 101st Airborne Division to protect the high school students from harm (C). These actions furthered civil rights by showing the government's defense of school integration.

18. D: The war ended during Nixon's administration, not during LBJ's term. The Great Society program included legislation to create Medicare (A), eliminate obstacles hindering the right to vote

(B), provide federal funding for education (C), and establish the Department of Housing and Urban Development (HUD). The Great Society also included a number of programs aimed at alleviating poverty. Johnson's social reform accomplishments were overshadowed by the Vietnam War during his last two years in office.

19. A: It is not true that the US captured Osama bin Laden shortly after the attacks. On October 7, the US attacked the Taliban regime in Afghanistan and defeated it in November, so these events did occur shortly after September 11, 2001, but bin Laden was not captured and killed until nearly ten years later, on May 2, 2011. It is true that Muslim terrorists flew two of the four American airplanes they had hijacked into the twin towers of the World Trade Center in New York City (B). They flew the third of the four planes into the US Department of Defense's headquarters, the Pentagon building in Arlington, Virginia, (C) near Washington, D.C. The fourth plane crashed in a field near Shanksville, Pennsylvania, after some of the passengers on board tried to overtake the terrorists (D). President George W. Bush announced a "war on terrorism" after these attacks killed a total of 2,995 people.

20. C: The rates of both productivity and inflation in the US were approximately 2% by 2000. By this time, the US economy was not increasing at a rate of 5% a year (A) but of 4% a year. Almost half of industrial growth contributing to economic prosperity was due to the "information revolution" made possible by the invention of the PC. The rate of unemployment in America at this time had not gone down to 6% (B) but to 4.7%. The stock market in the US had not just doubled in six years (D); it had actually quadrupled from 1992-1998 due to the increase in American households that owned stocks or bonds. Most of this ownership resulted from tax law changes regulating retirement accounts.

21. B: European immigration to America, the first event, hit a high in 1907, when 1,285,349 European immigrants came to America. The numbers were so great that Congress passed the Emergency Quota Act (A) in 1921. In order to implement greater restrictions on the influx of Southern and Eastern Europeans—particularly Jews, Italians, and Slavs—arriving in larger numbers since the 1890s, and even more as refugees before and during the Nazi and World War II years, Congress further passed the 1924 Immigration Act (C), which prohibited most European refugees from entering the United States. During the Great Depression (D) of the 1930s, immigration declined sharply due to the lack of economic opportunities.

22. D: All of these (D) events were associated with and/or had an impact on the emergence of the New Left, young people who were politically and socially disenchanted with America. In 1962, in Port Huron, Michigan, the SDS (A), spearheaded by Tom Hayden, Alan Huber, and others, held its first convention and was subsequently instrumental in student organization and advocacy for social and political reform (until 1969). The Berkeley Free Speech Movement (B) was organized at the University of California at Berkeley by student Mario Savio and others, insisting that the university's administrators remove their ban on campus political activity and recognize students' rights to free speech. The student activism generated by the Free Speech movement continues to this day, albeit not as rampantly as at the movement's inception. In 1968, when first Martin Luther King Jr. and then Robert Kennedy, both major leaders for reform, were assassinated (C), young people were further disaffected.

23. A: Roman civilization developed on the Tiber River, but it is not considered one of the earliest civilizations. Major civilizations developed along the other rivers listed: Chinese civilization developed in the Yangtze and Huang River valleys; Mesopotamian civilization emerged between the Tigris and Euphrates; and Egyptian culture developed in the Nile River valley.

24. D: The ancient Indus Valley civilization, also known in its mature phase as the Harappan civilization, existed in what now encompasses all of the listed countries today, except Turkey. This culture flourished from circa 2600–1900 BC, during the Bronze Age. This civilization included the most eastern portion of Balochistan in what is now Iran; the most western parts of what is now India; the majority of what is now Pakistan; and the southeastern part of Afghanistan.

25. B: Historians have determined that the Yellow River Valley in China began to develop into a cultural center during the Neolithic Era between c. 12,000–10,000 BC. The Shang Dynasty occurred between c. 1700–1046 BC—still part of the Ancient Era, but very long after the Neolithic era. The Xia Dynasty ruled between circa 2100–1600 BC, preceding the Shang Dynasty but still long after the Neolithic Era. Archaeological evidence exists of Homo erectus in China from more than a million years ago, during the Paleolithic Era, but the Yellow River Valley was not an emergent cultural center that long ago.

26. C: It is not true that Basil the Great was a leader in the West or that Benedict was a leader in the East with respect to early Christian monasticism. The reverse is true. St. Benedict was a leader of the monastic movement in the West, while Basil the Great was a monastic leader in the East. Initially, all monks were hermits, modeling their lifestyles on that of St. Anthony the Great (A). Eventually, perceiving the necessity of a spiritual organization, St. Pachomius created what would become the first monastery in 318 (B). St. Benedict created the code of spiritual practice, or rule, known as the Rule of St. Benedict, which became the most-followed rule during the middle ages (D).

27. D: All of these countries experienced their own Renaissances following the Italian Renaissance, which began in the cities of Florence and Siena and spread through Italy. From there the intellectual and cultural developments of the period spread to France from the late 15th to early 17th century, to Germany in the 15th and 16th centuries, and to England from the early 16th to early 17th century, as well as to the Netherlands in the 16th century, in a movement often known as the Northern Renaissance. This name distinguishes it from the original Italian Renaissance.

28. D: Power was centralized in the Incan Empire. When the invading Spaniards imprisoned Incan ruler Atahualpa and killed other Incan military leaders, the Incas were unable to mount an effective military response. Incas of lesser status simply lacked the appropriate authority. Answers A and B may be eliminated because they are factually inaccurate. The Incas had built some functional roads, which allowed the invading Spanish to access some Incan cities. Also, Pizarro's soldiers did not outnumber the Incans. The new diseases introduced by the Spanish decimated the Incan army, making D the correct answer. While the centralized power structure did create a vulnerability, the impact of disease was far more devastating.

29. D: All of these statements are correct regarding consequences of the French Revolution. French historian and political analyst Alexis de Tocqueville (famous for his book Democracy in America) saw the French Revolution as signifying the increasing social self-awareness of the middle class as it gained wealth (A). Conservative, anti-French Revolution philosopher and political theorist Edmund Burke believed that the Revolution was started by a small faction of conspirators who had no valid claims (B) for revolting and who brainwashed the public into subversive action against the status quo. Those persons who subscribe to Marxist philosophy focus on the rising up of the lower and middle working classes (C) against elite royalty who enjoyed unfair privileges.

30. A: Fascism was not opposed to nationalism and patriotism. Fascism was a radical political movement that was nationalistic in character. In fact, Fascism opposed Marxism (B) because Fascists saw Marxism as anti-nationalist and anti-patriotic. Fascism was both collectivist and saw itself as patriotic. Fascists were also against the bourgeoisie (B) for their individualism, which was the opposite of collectivism. Fascism did purport to be an alternative to Bolshevism (C). Nonetheless, despite this, the Fascist movement did have several things in common with Bolshevism (D). For example, both political movements believed in a single-party state, in appealing to the proletariat, and in the ruling over the masses by an elite group.

31. B: The country and population that moved out and relocated was the large population of Sephardic and Ashkenazi Jews in Algeria when that country became independent from France. The majority of these Algerian Jews evacuated Algeria and repatriated to France after the Second World War. The Chinese population in Singapore (A), the British population in Cayman Islands (C), and the Russian population in Kazakhstan (D) represent situations in which the longtime settler populations and the minority indigenous populations make decolonization impractical (even when the minority and majority are somewhat close in numbers).

32. B: Cars *were* included in the expectations of converting to atomic energy during the 1950s Nuclear Age. Not only were cars included in these projections, the Ford Motor Company actually presented a prototype of a nuclear-powered car, the Ford Nucleon Concept Car, in 1958. Although the model never went into production, the prototype and the concept remained as a symbol of the Nuclear Age. During the 1950s, the public attitude was one of nuclear optimism wherein nuclear power was viewed as overwhelmingly positive (A). People projected that in the future, the atomic bomb would take the place of all other earlier types of explosives (C). They also thought that nuclear power would replace the use of all other power sources such as coal and oil (D). People in 1950s America felt that nuclear power eventually would prove useful for almost everything, and that all applications of nuclear power would be beneficial.

33. D: Because the Puritans took on a Reformed theology, they were in this sense Calvinists. However, many Puritans endorsed radical views that criticized such Calvinists as John (Jean) Calvin and Huldrych (Ulrich) Zwingli in Switzerland. Not only were Puritans critical of Calvinists despite their mutual Reformed approaches, reciprocally many Calvinists were opposed to the Puritans as well. The Puritan movement changed less in American colonies than in England during the 1660s. Following the Restoration (1660) and the Uniformity Act (1662) in England, nearly all of the Puritan clergy objected and left the Church of England, thereby creating a dramatic change in the movement in that country. Nevertheless, in America, the Puritans who had emigrated from England continued their original Puritan traditions for a longer time, as they had neither the same Anglican Church as in England nor the legislation restoring earlier church status against which the English Puritans had reacted.

34. B: The witch hunts reflect a time when belief in magic and superstition was widespread. Many historians view them as a reaction to the social and economic changes of the Early Modern period.

35. C: Although options A, B, and D all describe important factors in the Neolithic Revolution, option C—the ability of communities to stockpile surplus food—is the factor most directly responsibility for the rise of trade practices. Communities were thus able to trade surplus food for other goods and services, a societal feature not present in hunter-gatherer societies. Option A, the ability of people to better choose where they lived (because they could carry the portable tools of agriculture with them to make a place habitable) contributed to the spread of agriculture, but less directly to the rise of trade practices. New advances in tools also contributed less directly to the rise of trade, as did the rise of new religious practices. These facts eliminate answers D and B, respectively.

36. D: Benjamin Franklin primarily served as an editor of the Declaration of Independence. Thomas Hobbes wrote about the idea of a Social Contract between government and the people that was used in the Declaration of Independence as a democratic principle in his *Leviathan* (1651), describing it in the context of an authoritarian monarchy. John Locke wrote about it in his *Second Treatise of Government* (1689), describing it in the context of a liberal monarchy. Jean-Jacques Rousseau wrote about it in his *Du Contrat Social*, or *The Social Contract* (1762), in the context of a liberal republic similar to what the new USA would become. These works supplied a theoretical basis for constitutional monarchies, liberal democracies, and republicanism.

37. A: The Navigation Acts in the seventeenth and eighteenth centuries restricted commercial activity in the American colonies and resulted in the constraint of manufacturing. The Acts were a logical extension of British mercantilism, a view according to which the colonies existed primarily to benefit Great Britain. Answer B can be rejected because one Navigation Act forced the colonists to buy more expensive sugar from the British West Indies, rather than the French West Indies. Option C can be eliminated because a positive result of the Navigation Acts was giving the American colonists a monopoly on tobacco by restricting tobacco production in Great Britain itself. Option D can be eliminated because the Acts did not place a tax on shipping goods to Great Britain.

38. C: The passage describes the 200-year period known as *Pax Romana.* Choice A is incorrect because the Julio-Claudian line held power in Rome for less than a century. Choice B refers to a succession of emperors that lasted less than one hundred years. The emperors in choice D only ruled from 69 AD to 96 AD.

39. D: The Angles and Saxons were two of the Germanic groups who competed for power after the fall of Rome. It is from them that the term Anglo-Saxons originated.

40. C: Fief refers to the section of land a lord might grant. Homage refers to the oath of loyalty the recipient of the land would make to the lord. Primogeniture refers to the system of inheritance that granted the son of a lord complete ownership and control of his landholdings. Vassal is the person who would receive land from the lord.

41. C: The main subject matter of civic responsibility is a person's responsibilities as a citizen. By contrast, the main subject matter of personal responsibility is one's responsibilities as a person. For example, keeping a promise to a friend is often a matter of personal responsibility because such a duty arises from the friendship. Serving on a jury when called to do so is an example of civic responsibility because such a duty arises from the person's citizenship. None of the other options given accurately describe the main subject matter of civic responsibility. For example, while a journalist might see accurate reporting of government actions as his or her civic responsibility, such reporting is not the main subject matter of civic responsibility and is also a responsibility that arises from that journalist's employment. Similar reasoning applies to a person's responsibilities as a government worker. This eliminates options A and D. Civic responsibility does not primarily concern inter-government relations; this eliminates option B.

42. B: President John Adams appointed William Marbury as Justice of the Peace, but Secretary of State James Madison never delivered the commission. Marbury claimed that under the Judiciary Act of 1789, the Supreme Court could order his commission be given to him. The Supreme Court denied Marbury's petition citing that the Judiciary Act of 1789 was unconstitutional, although they believed he was entitled to his commission.

43. D: The Bill of Rights was drafted by Congress to limit the authority of the government and protect the rights of individual citizens from abuse by the federal government. It was the first document to detail the rights of private citizens.

44. B: While the Senate needs a two-thirds or supermajority vote to ratify treaties, only a simple majority is necessary to pass a bill or confirm the appointments of the President.

45. B: Under the Fifth Amendment to the U.S. Constitution, the government may not strip certain basic rights from citizens without following the law. In the language of the Fifth Amendment itself, a person shall not "be deprived of life, liberty, or property without due process of law." Of all the options, option B is the only one that accurately describes the concept of due process as understood in the Fifth Amendment. Because due process does not explicitly guarantee a trial by jury within a reasonable timeframe, nor equal protection under the law (concepts covered elsewhere in the Constitution), options A and C can be rejected. Option D can be rejected because the Constitution restricts the government's ability to take away certain rights without following the law, not without a "dire cause" (such as the threat of imminent attack).

46. B: The Animal and Plant Health Inspection Service, the Food and Nutrition Service, and the Forest Service are agencies in the Department of Agriculture. The Department of Agriculture ensures food safety, works with farmers, promotes trade, and protects natural resources.

47. B: The House has strict rules that limit debate. A filibuster can only occur in the Senate where senators can speak on topics other than the bill at hand and introduce amendments. A filibuster can be ended by a supermajority vote of 60 senators.

48. C: The Government Accountability Office was originally called the General Accounting Office and was established in 1921 to audit the budget, Congress, and the Director of the Treasury. The Government Accountability Office now oversees the effectiveness of government spending in every branch.

49. A: Arbitration between organizations or individuals takes place in civil court. Civil trials are similar to criminal proceedings and require a jury. Both parties, however, can agree to let a judge decide the case.

50. D: Washington, D.C., as the US capitol, is a federal district. It has a local government in the form of a mayor and city council, but Congress has ultimate authority and can override the decisions made by the local government.

51. C: Tennessee was the only Southern state to ratify the 14th Amendment. Although Southern states that ratified this amendment could be readmitted to the Union with more reform, President Andrew Johnson, who was at odds with Congress, advised them against it.

52. C: The President must be a natural citizen, be at least 35 years old, and have lived in the US for 14 years. There is no education requirement for becoming President. Truman did not have a college education, but most Presidents have had college degrees.

53. B: Most presidents have only served two terms, a precedent established by George Washington. Ulysses S. Grant and Theodore Roosevelt sought third terms; however, only Franklin D. Roosevelt served more than two terms. He served a third term and won a fourth, but died in its first year. The 22nd Amendment was passed by Congress in 1947 and ratified in 1951. It officially limited the president to two terms, and a vice president who serves two years as president only can be elected for one term.

54. D: Minor parties often split from major parties and take voters with them. For example, Nader's Green Party was a spoiler in the 2000 election. Gore was down by 500 votes in Florida, and Nader had 100,000 votes in that state. The influence of minor parties on elections often forces the major parties to adjust their ideology.

55. A: Political socialization occurs when people are made aware of political culture, facts, and values. Family, friends, society, and the media influence political socialization. Sex, race, age, education, income, and region are also indicators of how a person will vote.

56. B: The Supreme Court ruled that statements made in interrogation are not admissible unless the defendant is informed of the right to an attorney and waives that right. The case of Miranda v. Arizona was consolidated with Westover v. United States, Vignera v. New York, and California v. Stewart.

57. B: All states have bicameral legislatures, except Nebraska. The bicameral legislatures in states resemble the federal legislature, with an upper house and a lower house.

58. D: Mount Kilimanjaro is not part of the Ring of Fire, a circle of volcanoes that stretches around the Pacific Ocean. The Ring of Fire extends from islands east of Australia through Indonesia, Japan, the Aleutian Islands connecting Russia to Alaska, and down the western coast of the Americas. It includes such famous volcanoes as Mount Saint Helens and Krakatoa. Over 90 percent of earthquakes and over 80 percent of volcanic eruptions occur along the Ring of Fire.

59. A: A smaller box in which some part of the larger map is depicted in greater detail is known as an inset. Insets provide a closer look at parts of the map that the cartographer deems to be more important (for instance, cities, national parks, or historical sites). Often, traffic maps will include several insets depicting the roads in the most congested area of the city. Legends, also known as keys, are the boxes in which the symbols used in the map are explained. A legend, or key, might indicate how railroads and boundaries are depicted, for example. A compass rose indicates how the map is oriented along the north-south axis. It is common for cartographers to tilt a map for ease of display, such that up may not be due north.

60. C: The shortest distance between New York and Paris goes near or over Labrador and Greenland. This is not apparent on a projection map, in which a straight line drawn between the two cities would extend straight out across the Atlantic Ocean, roughly along the 42nd parallel. The illusion that this straight line is the shortest path is a result of the distortions inherent in projection maps. On a globe, it would be easier to see that a plane flying from New York to Paris would cover the least ground by carving an arc, first up through eastern Canada and Greenland and then back down through the British Isles and northern France. This sort of path is known as a great circle route because it looks like an arc when it is drawn on a projection map.

61. C: Yemen is not a member of OPEC, the Organization of Petroleum Exporting Countries. Yemen has some deposits of oil, but the nation has only recently begun developing them. This, along with a desperate water shortage, accounts for Yemen's position as the poorest nation in the Middle East. OPEC was established in 1960 to set oil prices and production. Until the formation of OPEC, many oil-producing nations felt they were being exploited by Western oil companies. This organization has obtained a great deal of power and is held responsible for the gas shortages that wracked the United States during the late 1970s.

62. A: Antarctica will appear the largest on a Mercator projection. This projection map converts the globe into a rectangle, such that lines of longitude and latitude are perpendicular to one another. This type of map depicts landforms near the equator at nearly their normal size but increasingly stretches out distances as it reaches the poles. A Robinson projection, on the other hand, rounds the edges of the Mercator projection, such that the polar regions are not so large. A homolosine projection renders the sizes and shapes of landmasses correctly, but it distorts the distances between them. An azimuthal projection represents one hemisphere as a circle, such that a straight line from the center to any point on the map would also be the shortest distance in the real world.

63. C: The greatest area of corn production is in the United States, specifically in the so-called Corn Belt that runs from northern Florida and eastern Texas all the way up to Iowa and Pennsylvania. Corn has traditionally been the specialty grain of the Americas, although it is now grown as a subsistence crop all over the world. Indeed, all the incorrect answer choices are areas that produce significant amounts of corn, though not as much as the Corn Belt. Corn is useful because it can grow in various climates and can be converted into a number of different products.

64. C: In the plate movement known as subduction, an oceanic plate slides underneath a continental plate. Oceanic plates are denser, so they tend to go beneath when they are pressed against lighter continental plates. The edge of the oceanic plate will be melted by the earth's mantle and may reemerge as a volcano. The Cascade Range of the northwest United States was formed by subduction. In faulting, the edges of two plates grind against each other laterally. The San Andreas Fault in California is perhaps the most famous example of this process. In spreading, plates pull apart from each other, typically creating a rift valley and the potential for earthquakes. In converging, two plates of similar density press against each other, creating mountain ranges where they meet.

65. A: La Niña is a brief interval of coolness in between warm periods (El Niño) in the water of the Pacific Ocean. For a long time, La Niña was considered only in terms of its relation to El Niño. Increasingly, however, it is being studied as a climate event in its own right. A tropical gyre is a circle of winds made up of equatorial currents in one direction and countercurrents in the other direction. There are tropical gyres in both the Northern and Southern hemispheres. El Niño is an annual event, though some years it is considerably more pronounced. It is an increase in the temperature of coastal Pacific water, sometimes by as much as 2° Celsius. El Niño has a great impact on fishing and weather in the areas that border the Pacific Ocean. The El Niño–Southern Oscillation (ENSO) occurs during a particularly intense El Niño; the flow of equatorial wind and water during an ENSO actually reverses course.

66. C: Most early childhood experts believe that parents staying in children's bedrooms every night until the child falls asleep (choice A) can interfere with children's developing capacity to self-soothe. They advise parents to help young children, who often remain excited even when tired, to relax until they become sleepy, and then tell them "Good night" and "I love you" and leave the bedroom. While a minority of American parents currently endorse sleeping in family beds together with children, this practice is controversial and not preferred by most experts in the United States (D), though some also feel it does no harm. Regardless of sleeping practices, it is fairly common and normal for young children to have nightmares and/or nighttime fears. Experts advise that regardless of the individual family's choice of sleeping routines, it should be consistent to promote good sleeping habits in children. Inconsistent practices result in frustrated children and irregular sleep.

67. B: The Arab districts in North African cities are known as medinas. These are typically old neighborhoods surrounding a large mosque. Many Arabs who made their living in trade eventually settled in countries like Algeria, Tunisia, and Libya. There, they influenced culture by bringing Sunni Islam to the indigenous people. A souk, meanwhile, is a market area surrounding the mosque in the medina. A wadi is a dry North African creek bed, which becomes an essential source of water during the sporadic rains. The location of wadis has been a crucial factor in the political and economic history of North Africa. A bazaar, finally, is an open-air market in the Middle East.

68. D: The rocks and land formations that make up the earth's surface are collectively known as the lithosphere. The lithosphere does not include the core or mantle of the earth. The atmosphere is the air, water, and particles that are above the surface of the earth. The biosphere encompasses all the living things of the earth, such as animals, plants, fungi, and bacteria. The hydrosphere is all the water on and beneath the surface of the earth, including all the lakes, oceans, rivers, and creeks.

69. C: In the United States, geographers typically define a hamlet as a settlement with fewer than 100 inhabitants. A hamlet may have a few businesses, but it is unlikely to have a post office or a government office. A village is slightly larger than a hamlet; it may contain about 500 to 1,000 people. A village is likely to have a grocery store. A town is larger than a village. It usually has about 2,500 inhabitants. A city is larger than a town.

70. C: The cycle of demographic transition is best illustrated by a line graph. Demographic transition is a phenomenon in which a region's growth rate increases rapidly, peaks, and then decreases slowly over a long time. In the early phase of a region's development, both the birth and death rates are high, which can cause the population to fluctuate. As the people of the region become settled, the growth rate calms down, and the region enters a period of rapid increase. Political maps are better at depicting borders and the locations of cities, while pie charts are better at representing proportions. Flow-line maps are good for illustrating the movement of people, goods, or trends across a physical area.

71. D: The northernmost border between India and Pakistan is represented on political maps as a broken line because the borders of the Kashmir region remain in dispute. Both nations lay claim to this mountainous region, which has great water resources. This has been just one of the issues to complicate relations between these neighbors in South Asia. Although India controls most of Kashmir at present, the boundaries have not yet been fully resolved, and, on a political map, such undefined borders are usually represented with dotted lines.

72. A: Moldova is not one of the Baltic states. Latvia, Lithuania, and Estonia all border the Baltic Sea, which has enabled them to become major traders. Unfortunately, the smallness and advantageous locations of these nations has made them attractive to invaders. The Soviet Union took over these lands in 1939, and it was not until 1991 that they regained independence. All three of these nations are now struggling to establish themselves as viable economic actors.

73. C: The increasing popularity of Thai food in the United States is an example of cultural convergence, or the intersection of traits or customs from two distinct cultures. Thailand's cuisine has been introduced to the United States, but it has undergone subtle changes as a result of the desires and practices of the American consumer. The phenomenon of cultural convergence is credited with much of the innovation in any society. Cultural divergence, on the other hand, is the practice of shielding one culture from the influence of another. France, for instance, seeks to limit the influence of American culture on its citizens. Assimilation is the process by which a minority group gradually adopts the culture of the majority group. For example, many Native Americans assimilated into the European-style culture of the early American settlers. Acculturation is the process of obtaining the practices and ideas of a culture. A child undergoes acculturation, wherein he or she learns to think and act appropriately for his or her setting.

74. A: In geography, location—specifically, relative location—determines things like land prices based on the characteristics of an area, which are affected by nearby regions. An example of distance (B) is that land that is close to major highways is more expensive, while land far from main thoroughfares costs less. One example of pattern (C) in geography is that where rock folds form mountains (fold regions), the rivers accordingly form trellis patterns. Another example of pattern, in geographically oriented human behavior, is that settlements in mountainous areas form mainly spreading patterns. An example of interaction (D) in geography is when an industrial city needs raw materials from a rural village for production, and the village needs the city both as a market to buy its resources and for its industrial products: their mutual interdependence creates interaction between them.

75. D: When the FOMC sells bonds, they raise interest rates. This draws money out of the American economy, and attracts foreign investors. This causes the value of the American dollar to rise overseas, which makes American goods more expensive to overseas buyers and causes American exports to drop.

76. C: In the short-run Phillips curve, there is a trade-off between unemployment and inflation. There is no such trade-off in the long-run Phillips curve. According to the long-run Phillips curve, the economy tends to stay at the natural rate of unemployment, and any changes are minor variations that will self-correct.

77. D: Firms in a monopolistic competition are not efficient. They earn a profit above the minimum ATC, meaning they are not efficient productively, and they create output at a level less than the level of allocative efficiency.

78. A: Perfect competition is a theoretical type of market more so than one actually found in real life. That's because it is the most efficient, operating where P = MR = MC.

79. D: A market that is monopolistically competitive is relatively easy to enter and exit and has high levels of competition. Therefore, firms will enter and exit the market if it is not in long-run equilibrium. When price/quantity is below the minimum of the average total cost curve firms will exit the market.

80. B: Any expenditure that will increase a firm's future productivity is considered investment. Of the items listed, only the construction of a new plant matches the definition.

81. B: Nominal GDP is the total dollar value of goods and services produced in a country in a year. However, since prices increase with inflation, nominal GDP gives a skewed view of an economy when looking at various years over time. Therefore, economists multiply nominal GDP by a price deflator that accounts for inflation in order to arrive at real GDP.

82. D: In the long run, aggregate supply does not depend on price. Aggregate supply in the long run depends strictly on the amount of capital and labor and the type of available technology.

83. A: The Phillips Curve says that inflation and unemployment have an indirect relationship. If the Fed acts to stop inflation, then according to the Phillips Curve, unemployment will increase.

84. D: A change in productivity, such as workers becoming more or less productive, would affect how many goods can be supplied. No change in worker productivity would cause no change in AS. Choices A, B, and C would all affect input prices and therefore would all affect AS.

85. B: The multiplier effect states that a given increase in spending, when multiplied by the multiplier, will lead to a given increase in AD. In this case, the $1,000,000 spending increase and the multiplier of 5 lead to an AD increase of $5,000,000 ($1,000,000 × 5 = $5,000,000).

86. C: Answers A, B, and D are all correct. However, if the government imposes a tax on a good with a highly inelastic demand, producers can shift a lot of the cost of the tax onto consumers, since demand does not vary much as price increases.

87. B: When AD for the goods produced by an industry decreases, one might expect the wages paid to workers in that industry to decrease as a result. However, because unions negotiate contracts with employers, wages of unionized workers tend not to fall in these circumstances. This tendency for wages to stay the same is known as "sticky wages."

88. A: The Consumer Price Index is the value of a "market basket" of goods and services in one year compared to the value of the same goods and services in another year.

89. A: The nominal interest rate is stated interest rate, while the real interest rate is the nominal interest rate adjusted for inflation. If prices decrease during the period of the loan, the real interest rate will be less than the nominal interest rate.

90. B: The current account is part of what makes up a country's balance of payment account. The current account records the value of exports and imports of goods and services by a country, the country's net investment income, and the country's net transfers.

Practice Test #2

1. Which of the following Native American peoples would early European explorers NOT have encountered on their visits to the West Indies?

a. Totonacs
b. Ciboney
c. Caribs
d. Tainos

2. Which of the following was the reason the economy of colonial New England focused mainly on manufacture and trade?

a. The soil and climate conditions in New England were not conducive to year-round farming.
b. The New England colonists were primarily merchants from England and Scotland.
c. Slavery did not exist in the northern colonies.
d. The New England colonists wanted to achieve economic dominance over the Middle Atlantic colonies.

3. The idea that the purpose of the American colonies was to provide Great Britain with raw materials and a market for its goods is an expression of:

a. Free trade
b. Most favored nation status
c. Mercantilism
d. Laissez-faire capitalism

4. Which of these states was NOT one of the original 13 colonies?

a. Maine
b. Rhode Island
c. New Hampshire
d. New Jersey

5. Which statement best describes the significance of the Mayflower Compact on colonial America?

a. It declared that the colonists were independent from King James.
b. It served as a blueprint for the later Bill of Rights.
c. It provided the Pilgrims the first written basis for laws in the New World.
d. It established Puritanism as the official religion for Puritan colonies.

6. Which act of Parliament angered the American colonists without raising the issue of unfair taxation?

a. The Sugar Act
b. The Stamp Act
c. The Quartering Act
d. The Townshend Acts

7. The following lines were written by Paul Revere in 1770:

Unhappy Boston! See thy sons deplore
Thy hallowed walks besmear'd with guiltless gore.
While faithless Preston and his savage bands,
With murderous rancor stretch their bloody hands;
Like fierce barbarians grinning o'er their prey,
Approve the carnage and enjoy the day.

What was the event that inspired these words?

a. The Boston Massacre
b. The Boston Tea Party
c. The midnight ride of Paul Revere
d. The Battle of Lexington and Concord

8. Article I of the United States Constitution includes the following paragraph:

No title of nobility shall be granted by the United States: and no person holding any office of profit or trust under them, shall, without the consent of the Congress, accept of any present, emolument, office, or title, of any kind whatever, from any king, prince, or foreign state.

This paragraph most directly reflects the influence of which of the following people?

a. John Locke
b. Baron de Montesquieu
c. Jean-Jacques Rousseau
d. Thomas Paine

9. Under the Articles of Confederation, which of the following was Congress NOT granted the power to do?

a. Wage war and make treaties
b. Regulate Indian affairs
c. Appoint military officers
d. Levy taxes

10. Who was the main author of the Bill of Rights?

a. George Washington
b. John Adams
c. Thomas Jefferson
d. James Madison

11. Which of the following best describes the annexation of Texas by the United States in 1845?

a. An effort to help stem the spread of slavery west of the Mississippi
b. Part of an effort to fulfill Manifest Destiny
c. An expression of principles set forth in the Monroe Doctrine
d. An effort to improve relations between the United States and Mexico

12. The Wilmot Proviso, which would have prohibited slavery in any territory acquired from Mexico, was favored by the North and bitterly opposed by the South. The issue was resolved by means of which of the following?

a. A Supreme Court decision
b. The Missouri Compromise
c. The Compromise of 1850
d. The Kansas-Nebraska Act

13. The two new states admitted under the Missouri Compromise of 1820 were Missouri and what other state?

a. Ohio
b. Alabama
c. Kansas
d. Maine

14. Which of the following territories was acquired last by the United States?

a. The Texas Annexation
b. Oregon Country
c. The Gadsden Purchase
d. The Mexican Cession

15. Which events are correctly paired to show cause and effect?

a. The Spanish-American War → the US annexation of Hawaii
b. The assassination of William McKinley → the decline of US imperialism
c. The Russo-Japanese War → the Boxer Rebellion
d. The Platt Amendment → the establishment of the US naval base at Guantanamo Bay

16. The end of Reconstruction was marked by which event?

a. The assassination of Abraham Lincoln
b. Ratification of the 14th Amendment
c. The impeachment of Andrew Johnson
d. The withdrawal of federal troops from the South

17. Although Roosevelt's New Deal solved many problems, it also did which of the following?

a. Failed to provide direct relief to the poor
b. Had little effect on the problem of unemployment
c. Raised the national debt
d. Weakened labor unions

18. Which of the following was a major cause of the Great Depression of the 1930s?

a. The overproduction and underconsumption of consumer goods
b. The failure of industry to produce sufficient consumer goods
c. Underproduction and rising prices in the agricultural sector
d. The reduction of import tariffs

19. Following World War I, African Americans migrated in great numbers to the north for what reason?

a. New federal laws banned employment discrimination in the northern states.
b. Returning African-Americans veterans were not used to the rural economy of the South.
c. Greater job opportunities were available in northern cities.
d. Northern states had passed laws to assure equal voting rights for all Americans.

20. The reforms set in motion by the Russian leader Mikhail Gorbachev played an important role in which of the following?

a. The breakup of the Soviet Union
b. Creating economic prosperity in post-Cold War Russia
c. Prolonging the Cold War
d. Ending the war in Bosnia

21. The strategy of containment was a major element of American foreign policy during:

a. The Spanish-American War
b. World War I
c. World War II
d. The Cold War

22. Which of the following was NOT a prominent poet of the Harlem Renaissance?

a. Zora Neale Hurston
b. Countee Cullen
c. Langston Hughes
d. James Weldon Johnson

23. Put the following events in order from oldest to most recent.

1) Martin Luther King led the March on Washington.
2) Brown v. Board of Education overturned the policy of "separate but equal" education.
3) The Student Non-Violent Coordinating Committee began staging sit-ins at segregated lunch counters in the South.
4) The arrest of Rosa Parks sparked the Montgomery Bus Boycott.

a. 2,4,3,1
b. 1,3,2,4
c. 3,4,1,2
d. 2,1,4,3

24. Which of the following BEST describes the significance of the US Supreme Court's decision in the Dred Scott case?

a. The ruling effectively declared slavery to be a violation of the Constitution.
b. The ruling guaranteed full citizenship rights to freed slaves.
c. The ruling turned many Southerners against the Supreme Court.
d. The ruling furthered the gap between North and South and hastened the Civil War.

25. Unlike slaves, who were considered to be the property of their masters, which of the following was true regarding most indentured servants in colonial times?

a. They received wages for their labor
b. They were generally treated kindly by their employers
c. They were highly educated
d. They voluntarily entered into servitude

26. With the end of Reconstruction in 1877, which of the following was true regarding African Americans in the South?

a. They soon took control of state legislatures
b. They formed a new political party to protect their own interests
c. They were able to rise quickly into the economic middle class
d. They were kept from voting by poll taxes and literacy tests

27. In 1978, President Jimmy Carter met with leaders of which two nations to broker the Camp David Accords?

a. China and the Soviet Union
b. Israel and Egypt
c. Iran and Iraq
d. North Korea and South Korea

28. Of the following economists, who advocated government intervention to prevent and remedy recessions and depressions?

a. Adam Smith
b. John Maynard Keynes
c. Friedrich Hayek
d. Milton Friedman

29. Which of these was the greatest obstacle to success for the farmers who settled on the Great Plains in the latter part of the nineteenth century?

a. The invention of barbed wire
b. Passage of the Homestead Act
c. Environmental conditions
d. The Grange movement

30. In 1970, several student demonstrators were killed at Kent State University in Ohio and Jackson State College in Mississippi. What were the students protesting?

a. The election of Richard Nixon
b. The suppression of free speech on campus
c. The bombing of Cambodia
d. The incursion into Laos

31. Which of these was NOT an immediate consequence of the Age of Exploration?

a. The development of more accurate navigation instruments
b. The introduction of new foods and other goods to Europe
c. The decline of England as a world power
d. The discovery of new lands where people might seek a better life

32. The first ships to set sail from Europe in the Age of Exploration departed from which country?

a. Spain
b. The Netherlands
c. England
d. Portugal

33. A group that grew in numbers as a result of the Industrial Revolution was:

a. Small farmers.
b. Unskilled workers.
c. Skilled craftsmen.
d. The rural population.

34. Which of the following is a secondary source of information about World War II?

a. A Ph.D. dissertation comparing World War II and the war in Vietnam
b. A diary written by a soldier during the Battle of the Bulge
c. A battlefield map found in a German tank in 1939
d. The front page of the December 7, 1941 edition of the New York Times

35. The purpose of the Dayton Accords of 1995 was to resolve the bloody conflict in which of the following nations?

a. Bosnia
b. Kosovo
c. Albania
d. Croatia

36. Which one of these landmark Supreme Court decisions involving the right to an attorney took place sometime after the Cold War?

a. *Gideon v. Wainwright*
b. *Montejo v. Louisiana*
c. *Escobedo v. Illinois*
d. *Miranda v. Arizona*

37. During the 15th century, Johann Gutenberg invented a printing press with moveable type. How did his invention influence science?

a. It did not influence science; the printing of Gutenberg Bibles directed public attention away from science and toward reforming the Catholic Church.
b. It led to scientific advances throughout Europe by spreading scientific knowledge.
c. It influenced scientific advancement in Germany only, where Gutenberg's press was based.
d. It did not influence science; though texts with scientific knowledge were printed, distribution of these texts was limited.

38. A monotheistic religious practice was central to which of the following cultures?

a. Egyptians
b. Hebrews
c. Sumerians
d. Babylonians

39. The Maastricht Treaty of 1992 removed many of the economic and political barriers that existed among members of which of the following groups?

a. United Nations
b. North Atlantic Treaty Organization
c. European Union
d. Organization of Petroleum Exporting Countries

40. NAFTA was replaced by the USMCA in 2020. Which of the following nations is NOT a member of these agreements?

a. Mexico
b. Brazil
c. the United States
d. Canada

41. According to Karl Marx, which two groups are in continual conflict?

a. Farmers and landowners
b. Workers and owners
c. Kings and nobles
d. Politicians and voters

42. In writing the sole dissenting opinion in a famous Supreme Court case, Justice John Marshall Harlan wrote these words:

> Our Constitution is color-blind, and neither knows nor tolerates classes among citizens. In respect of civil rights, all citizens are equal before the law.

What was the case about which he was writing?

a. Marbury v. Madison
b. Plessy v. Ferguson
c. Gideon v. Wainwright
d. Brown v. Board of Education

43. When state legislatures pass laws that regulate driving, marriage, and public education, they are exercising which of the following?

a. Implied, or suggested, powers
b. Shared, or concurrent, powers
c. Expressed, or enumerated, powers
d. Reserved powers

44. The power of Congress to regulate interstate commerce was the main issue argued in which of the following historic cases?

a. Marbury v. Madison
b. Dartmouth College v. Woodward
c. McCulloch v. Maryland
d. Gibbons v. Ogden

45. The First Amendment to the Constitution deals mainly with which of the following?

a. The right to free expression
b. The right to a speedy and public trial
c. Protection from cruel and unusual punishment
d. Freedom from unreasonable search and seizure

46. The principle that freedom of speech can be limited when the exercise of that freedom creates "a clear and present danger" was established in which Supreme Court decision?

a. Plessy v. Ferguson (1896)
b. Schenck v. United States (1919)
c. Engle v. Vitale (1962)
d. Miranda v. Arizona (1966)

47. The trial of John Peter Zenger in 1735 laid the groundwork for which amendment to the Constitution?

a. The First Amendment
b. The Second Amendment
c. The Third Amendment
d. The Fourth Amendment

48. Under the United States Constitution, the power to tax and borrow is:

a. Implied
b. Shared
c. Expressed
d. Reserved

49. Which of the following accurately describes the process by which government officials may be impeached and removed from office?

a. Charges are brought by the House of Representatives and tried in the Senate.
b. Charges are brought by the Senate and tried in the House of Representatives.
c. Charges are brought by the Attorney-General and tried in Congress.
d. Charges are brought by both houses of Congress and tried in the Supreme Court.

50. What is the power of the President to veto an act of Congress an example of?

a. Checks and balances
b. Separation of powers
c. Judicial review
d. Advice and consent

51. How can Congress override the presidential veto of a bill?

a. By a majority vote in the House and a two-thirds majority in the Senate
b. By a two-thirds vote in the House and a majority in the Senate
c. By a majority vote in both the House and the Senate
d. By a two-thirds vote in both the House and the Senate

52. Which of the following is NOT an example of a shared, or concurrent, power?

a. The power to build roads
b. The power to coin money
c. The power to collect taxes
d. The power to establish courts

53. What was the immediate result of the Lincoln-Douglas debates?

a. Lincoln's election to the United States Senate
b. Douglas's election to the United States Senate
c. Lincoln's election to the Illinois State Senate
d. Lincoln's election as President of the United States

54. What is the main purpose of the census?

a. To monitor illegal immigration
b. To apportion seats in the House of Representatives
c. To help determine federal income tax rates
d. To reapportion seats in the United States Senate

55. The Seneca Falls Convention of 1848 marked the beginning of which of the following?

a. Abolitionist movement
b. Republican Party
c. Temperance movement
d. Women's rights movement

56. Which of the following was a book that influenced Congress to pass the Food and Drug Act of 1906?

a. *The Octopus* by Frank Norris
b. *How the Other Half Lives* by Jacob Riis
c. *The Jungle* by Upton Sinclair
d. *The Shame of the Cities* by Lincoln Steffens

57. The Federal Deposit Insurance Corporation (FDIC) and the Securities and Exchange Commission (SEC) were created during whose presidency?

a. Theodore Roosevelt
b. Woodrow Wilson
c. Franklin Roosevelt
d. Harry Truman

58. A theory of the late 19th century that strongly opposed governmental interference in economic affairs was known as which of the following?

a. Popularism
b. Utopian Socialism
c. Progressivism
d. Social Darwinism

59. Which of the following is true regarding the Tropic of Capricorn?

a. It separates the northern and southern hemispheres.
b. It separates the eastern and western hemispheres.
c. It is the southernmost latitude at which the sun can appear directly overhead at noon.
d. It is the northernmost latitude at which the sun can appear directly overhead at noon.

Refer to the following for question 60:

For a geography unit, students are learning about the state of Wisconsin. To help better understand the climate of the state, students are asked to record how the elevation of certain regions correlates to temperature. They are also expected to locate and label the major cities of the state, such as Madison and Milwaukee.

60. What would be the best map to use to find the highest elevation in Wisconsin?

a. Political map
b. Topographic map
c. Resource map
d. Road map

61. If you know the longitude of a city in the United States, what can you determine?

a. The state in which it is located
b. The time zone in which it is located
c. Exactly how far it is from the equator
d. Approximate average winter temperature

62. Which of these statements about Africa is true?

a. It is nearly twice the size of the continental United States.
b. It includes about 20 percent of the world's land surface but only 16 percent of its population.
c. Almost the entire continent lies south of the equator.
d. Nearly 50 percent of southern Africa consists of rain forest.

63. The physical geography of a region most directly affects which of the following?

a. The religious beliefs of the native population
b. The family structure of the native population
c. The dietary preferences of the native population
d. The language spoken by the native population

64. Which of the following is the LEAST useful in controlling soil erosion?

a. Crop rotation
b. Cattle grazing
c. Mulching
d. Reforestation

65. Which biome is NOT found in the Torrid Zone?

a. Desert
b. Savanna
c. Rainforest
d. Taiga

66. Most of the region known in ancient times as Mesopotamia is located in which present-day nation?

a. Iran
b. Saudi Arabia
c. Turkmenistan
d. Iraq

67. Which of the following is an example of chemical weathering?

a. Frost wedging
b. Heat expansion
c. Acid rain
d. Salt wedging

68. Which of these countries does NOT share a land border with Israel?

a. Jordan
b. Saudi Arabia
c. Lebanon
d. Egypt

69. Which of the following is NOT one of the criteria for nationhood?

a. Defined territory
b. Elections
c. Government
d. Sovereignty

70. Carrie Chapman Catt founded the League of Women Voters in 1920 in response to which of the following historical events?

a. The election of President Woodrow Wilson.
b. The passage of the Nineteenth Amendment to the Constitution.
c. The breakup of the National Women's Party.
d. The end of World War I.

71. Dr. Michael DeBakey is known mainly for his contributions to which field?

a. Neurology
b. Cardiology
c. Psychiatry
d. Oncology

72. A society produces 10 units of Good X and 10 units of Good Y. Then, the society changes its production, increasing production of Good X to 15 units. Production of Good Y drops to 6 units. What is the opportunity cost of producing the additional 5 units of Good X?

a. 5 units of Good X
b. 15 units of Good X
c. 6 units of Good Y
d. 4 units of Good Y

73. The economic theories of John Maynard Keynes are most closely associated with which of the following?

a. The view that deficit spending leads to inflation
b. Advocating government action against monopolies
c. The view that supply creates its own demand
d. Advocating government action to stimulate economic growth

74. The US government seeks to reduce unemployment in part to prevent individuals from suffering hardship. How is unemployment also most likely to affect the economy in the short run?

a. By causing inflation
b. By leading to lost productivity
c. By increasing aggregate demand
d. By increasing aggregate supply

75. Which of the following is included in the unemployment rate typically followed by economists?

I. Structural unemployment
II. Frictional unemployment
III. Cyclical unemployment

a. I only
b. II only
c. III only
d. I and II only

76. Assume that aggregate demand (AD) decreases. How will this decrease affect real GDP if there is a lot of unemployment as opposed to full employment?

a. If there is a lot of unemployment, prices will rise dramatically.
b. If there is a lot of unemployment, GDP will stay the same.
c. If there is full employment, GDP will increase dramatically.
d. If there is a lot of unemployment, GDP will decrease.

77. Consider the graph below. Which of the following is true?

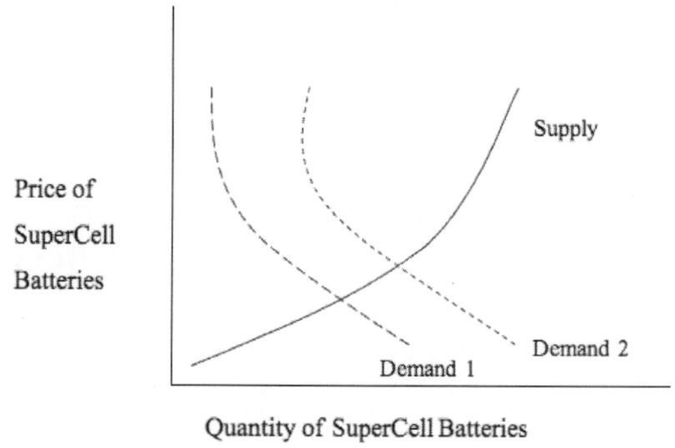

a. The price has decreased with a shift in supply.
b. The equilibrium point has remained constant.
c. The price has risen with a shift in demand.
d. There a double coincidence of wants.

78. Which of the following was a stated reason for Jefferson's opposition to the Bank of the United States?

a. He did not think the Bank would effectively further his goal of establishing a strong central government.
b. He was a strict constructionist.
c. He believed the Bank would give an unfair advantage to the southern states.
d. He distrusted the fiscal policies of the Democratic-Republicans.

79. What is the main reason that the Federal Reserve Board lowers interest rates?

a. To lower prices
b. To stimulate consumer spending
c. To encourage international trade
d. To control inflation

80. Who was the economist focused on the potential for populations to grow faster than available food supplies?

a. Adam Smith
b. John Stuart Mill
c. Thomas Malthus
d. Friedrich Engels

81. Which of the following could best be used in order to determine the "price deflator" for converting nominal GDP to real GDP?

a. Consumer Price Index
b. Gross National Product
c. Business Cycle
d. Phillips Curve

82. Sally's grandmother kept $100,000 in a cookie jar for years but recently gave it to Sally, who immediately puts it in her bank in a savings account. The bank has a 20% reserve rate. Which of the following is true?

I. Excess reserves increase by $20,000
II. The bank's money supply increases by as much as $120,000
III. There is no change in the bank's money supply

a. I only
b. I and II
c. III
d. None of the above

83. Which of the following are the leading producers of petroleum in Latin America?

a. Argentina and Bolivia
b. Mexico and Guatemala
c. Brazil and Venezuela
d. Colombia and Uruguay

84. An increase in the value of the American dollar in foreign exchange markets might be caused by what?

a. An increase in aggregate demand (AD) in the US
b. An increase in interest rates in the US
c. A balance of payments that equals zero (debits equal credits)
d. Inflation in the US

85. The social scientists most likely to study the role of kinship relationships within a cultural group are:

a. Economists
b. Political scientists
c. Psychologists
d. Anthropologists

86. Which of these presidents most greatly expanded the power of the presidency?

a. Thomas Jefferson
b. Herbert Hoover
c. Lyndon Johnson
d. Ronald Reagan

87. Middle-grades students are expected to communicate in written, oral, and visual forms. To meet this expectation, it will be most important for students to have developed the ability to do which of the following?

a. Differentiate between primary and secondary sources
b. Translate information from one medium to another
c. Apply procedures for problem solving and decision making
d. Identify bias in written, oral, and visual material

88. Which social science focuses primarily on how a society produces and distributes goods?

a. Sociology
b. Anthropology
c. Psychology
d. Economics

89. A historian is writing a book about George W. Bush's years as governor of Texas. All of the information she uses is derived from original public records, Bush's personal letters, and interviews she conducted with various government officials who served during his administration. Which of the following is the historian's book based?

a. Only on primary sources
b. Only on secondary sources
c. Mostly on secondary sources
d. Equally on primary and secondary sources

90. As an archeologist and paleoanthropologist, Louis Leakey was mainly interested in which of the following?

a. Investigating social relationships among the indigenous people of Kenya
b. Searching for the remains of extinct animal species
c. Studying the fossil record to investigate human origins
d. Analyzing the economic and political traditions of eastern Africa

Answer Key and Explanations for Test #2

1. A: While the Ciboney, Caribs, and Tainos were indigenous to the islands of the West Indies, the Totonacs lived in Mexico. They are sometimes credited with founding the ancient city of Teotihuacan.

2. A: Agriculture was not a viable economic model for New Englanders. Although the colonists were mainly from England and Scotland, few were merchants before arriving in the colonies. Slavery existed in the north, although it was less important to the economy than it was in the agricultural south. New England colonists were not actively competing with their neighbors to the immediate south.

3. C: Mercantilism is the economic theory that nations advance the goal of accumulating capital by maintaining a balance of trade such that the value of exports exceeds that of imports. Great Britain maintained colonies to provide an inexpensive source of raw materials while creating markets for the goods manufactured in England. Under free trade, governments refrain from hindering the international exchange of goods and services. Nations that are granted most favored nation status are assured of enjoying equal advantages in international trade. A laissez-faire capitalist economy would theoretically be completely free of government regulation.

4. A: Maine was the northern part of the Massachusetts Bay colony and subsequently part of the Commonwealth of Massachusetts. It became a state in 1820 as a result of the Missouri Compromise.

5. C: The male passengers of the Mayflower signed the Compact after a disagreement regarding where in the Americas they should establish a colony. The Compact served as a written basis for laws in their subsequent colony. Because the Mayflower Compact did not list particular rights, it is not best understood as a blueprint for the Bill of Rights. This eliminates choice B. Though the Compact did in part serve as a basis for government, it did not declare independence from King James; its last line, for example, specifically refers to King James as the writers' sovereign. This eliminates choice A. Finally, although the Mayflower Compact does include religious language, it is a brief document that does not detail, defend, or establish as official any particular religious doctrine, including Puritan religious doctrine. This eliminates choice D.

6. C: The Quartering Act required colonists to provide food and shelter to British soldiers. Unlike the other mentioned acts, it did not impose a tax on sugar, coffee, tea, printed materials, or other items in common use by the colonists.

7. A: On March 5, 1770 angry colonists in Boston threw snowballs at a British officer. The violence quickly escalated, and the soldiers commanded by Captain Preston eventually fired on the crowd and killed several people. The silversmith and engraver Paul Revere engraved a depiction of the event and wrote an inflammatory poem to accompany his engraving. The Boston Tea Party took place over three years later. Revere's famous ride to announce the movement of the British army took place in 1775, and the Battle of Lexington and Concord, which was the first military engagement of the American Revolution, was fought the same day.

8. D: In his extremely influential pamphlet *Common Sense*, Paine argued persuasively against all forms of monarchy and aristocracy. He advocated the formation of a republic that derives its power exclusively from the governed. While the European writers also advocated government that derives its authority from the people, none went as far as Paine in proposing the total abolition of the traditional noble classes.

9. D: Without the power of taxation, the new federal government had to rely on the states to provide the money needed to wage war against England and to pay the huge national debt accrued during the Revolution. The power to raise revenues through taxation was an essential feature of the subsequent Constitution.

10. D: Madison proposed 19 amendments to the first Congress in 1789. 12 of these were sent to the states and 10 were officially ratified in 1791. Neither Adams nor Jefferson was present at the Constitutional Convention.

11. B: The term "Manifest Destiny" originated with the annexation of Texas as Americans began to envision a nation that spread from coast to coast. Texas entered the union as a slave state. The Monroe Doctrine addressed European intervention in the Western Hemisphere, which was not an issue in the annexation of Texas. Mexican resentment of the annexation was a factor in the Mexican War, which began the following year.

12. C: The Compromise of 1850 admitted California as a free state while the territories of Utah and New Mexico would decide for themselves whether to be slave or free. The compromise also prohibited the trading of slaves in D.C. while making it easier for slave owners to recover fugitive slaves. The Missouri Compromise of 1820 addressed the issue of slavery in the Louisiana Purchase. The Kansas-Nebraska Act of 1854 repealed the Missouri Compromise and created the territories of Kansas and Nebraska.

13. D: Under the Missouri Compromise, Maine would be admitted as a free state while Missouri would enter as a slave state. Slavery would be prohibited in the former Louisiana Territory north of the 36°30' parallel except in the new state of Missouri. Ohio had entered the Union in 1803 under the Northwest Ordinance. Alabama had been admitted as a slave state shortly before the Missouri Compromise. After years of bloody conflict, Kansas entered the Union as a free state in 1861.

14. C: The Gadsden Purchase of 1853 added a small strip of Mexican land in southern Arizona and New Mexico that provided a valuable railroad route to California. Texas was annexed in 1845. The Oregon border dispute between the United States and Great Britain was settled in 1846. The Mexican Cession was part of the Treaty of Guadalupe Hidalgo in 1848.

15. D: The Platt Amendment of 1901 granted the United States the right to intervene in Cuban affairs and maintain a presence on the island. Hawaii was annexed during the Spanish-American War, though the war was not a direct cause of it. US imperialism was accelerated following McKinley's assassination. The Boxer Rebellion took place in China between 1899 and 1901 and preceded the Russo-Japanese War, which began in 1904.

16. D: The last federal troops were removed from the South in 1877 following the inauguration of Republican President Rutherford B. Hayes. The goals of reunifying the country and establishing functional state governments in the South were not marked by Lincoln's assassination in 1865, ratification of the 14th Amendment in 1868, or the 1868 impeachment of Andrew Johnson.

17. C: To achieve Roosevelt's goals, a great deal of money had to be spent, and the national debt skyrocketed. Millions of poor families received welfare, many jobs were created, and labor unions were strengthened with passage of the National Labor Relations Act.

18. A: Along with stock market speculation, a major cause of the Great Depression was an increased supply of cars, radios, and other goods that was not matched by consumer demand. Industrial production far exceeded the population's purchasing power. Farmers were plagued by overproduction and falling prices while international trade suffered from rising tariffs.

19. C: World War I sparked a frenzy of production in the factories of Chicago, New York, and other northern cities, and a decrease in European immigration created a serious labor shortage. Workers from the South were actively recruited by factory owners. The federal government did not interfere with discriminatory hiring practices until long after World War I, and the Voting Rights Act was not passed until 1965. African-American veterans from the South returned to the same rural economy in which they had grown up.

20. A: In 1985, Mikhail Gorbachev's programs of "glasnost," or openness, and "perestroika," or economic restructuring, led to an increase in free speech and free enterprise throughout the Soviet Union. By 1991, these reforms had led to the collapse of Communist power in Russia and the dissolution of the Soviet Union. Russia and the other newly independent states that comprised the former Soviet Union suffered great economic hardship following the breakup. With the collapse of the Soviet Union as a world power, the Cold War that began after World War II came to an end. The bloody conflict in Bosnia (1992-1995) was caused in part by the weakening of Communist control in Yugoslavia at the end of the Cold War.

21. D: Formulated during the Truman administration and enduring throughout the Cold War, the policy of containment was intended to prevent the spread of Communism after World War II. It served as a rationale for many military decisions during the Korean and Vietnamese conflicts.

22. A: Hurston (1891-1960) achieved great acclaim as a novelist, playwright, short story writer, and essayist during the Harlem Renaissance that blossomed in New York City from around 1919 to the mid-1930s. Cullen, Hughes, and Johnson were among the movement's best-known poets.

23. A: Brown v. Board of Education was decided in 1954. Rosa Parks was arrested in 1955. The lunch counter sit-ins were staged in 1960. The March on Washington took place in 1963.

24. D: In the Dred Scott decision of 1857, the Court ruled that no slave or descendant of slaves could ever be a United States citizen. It also declared the Missouri Compromise of 1820 to be unconstitutional, clearing the way for the expansion of slavery in new American territories. This ruling pleased Southerners and outraged the North, further dividing the nation and setting the stage for war.

25. D: Indentured servants agreed to work for a set period of time in exchange for transportation to the New World and such basic necessities as food and shelter. They did not receive wages and were generally not highly-educated people. Employers often viewed indentured servants with scorn and treated them as harshly as they treated slaves.

26. D: Although the Thirteenth, Fourteenth, and Fifteenth Amendments guaranteed certain legal protection to African Americans, Southern whites were able to retain power by enacting various restrictions on voting. Lacking formal education and deprived of their right to vote, freed slaves were unable to attain political or economic power in the South.

27. B: Israeli Prime Minister Menachem Begin and Egyptian President Anwar El Sadat negotiated for twelve days at Camp David in Maryland before reaching the agreements that led to the Israel-Egypt Peace Treaty of 1979. The agreement called for Israeli withdrawal from the Sinai Peninsula and represented the possibility of future compromise between Israel and its Arab neighbors.

28. B: Keynesian economics is based on the notion that governments can effectively stimulate economic growth through taxation, adjustment of interest rates, and the funding of public projects. His economic philosophy contrasts sharply with the free-market philosophies of Smith, Hayek, and Friedman.

29. C: Nature imposed great hardships on farmers. Drought, wind, fires, blizzards, and subzero temperatures made life on the plains very difficult and dangerous. The invention of barbed wire in 1874 allowed farmers to keep livestock from damaging their crops. The Homestead Act of 1862 encouraged settlement of the west and made land available to some 600,000 homesteaders. Founded in 1867, the Grange united farmers in their effort to regulate storage and shipping costs and generally protect their own interests.

30. C: In 1970, American forces joined South Vietnamese troops in an attack on Communist bases in Cambodia. This extension of the war in Vietnam outraged not only college students but many of their elders as well. Nixon was elected in 1968, and the incursion into Laos occurred the year after Cambodia was bombed. The Free Speech Movement was organized in Berkeley and was not directly linked to the demonstrations in Ohio and Mississippi.

31. C: Exploration between the 15th and 17th centuries resulted in contact between European cultures and many previously unknown or little-known cultures. Navigation techniques improved, food and other goods were imported, and the New World began to be settled. Rather than declining in influence, England became a more prominent imperial power during this era.

32. D: The Portuguese prince called Henry the Navigator launched the Age of Exploration with his voyage of 1419. He was followed by such notable Portuguese sailors as Bartolomeu Dias and Vasco da Gama, but Portuguese fortunes waned in the ensuing centuries as Spanish and Dutch exploration gained prominence.

33. B: As production shifted to factories, a large number of unskilled workers were needed to operate the machinery that was beginning to put many skilled craftsmen out of work. As farms grew larger and increasingly mechanized, the number of people who owned their own farm began to decrease. The rural population declined as people flocked to the cities in search of employment.

34. A: A secondary source is a document that discusses or analyzes information that was originally presented elsewhere. While a Ph.D. dissertation may use primary sources to make its case, it is generally based on an analysis of previous texts. A dissertation that mentions the Vietnam conflict had to have been written subsequent to World War II. The other choices all represent primary sources that are contemporary to the war.

35. A: Nationalistic conflicts arose in 1991 when Slovenia and Croatia declared independence from Yugoslavia. A civil war between Croatians and Serbians was followed by an outbreak of violence between Serbians and the Muslims of Bosnia-Herzegovina. In 1995, leaders of Bosnia, Croatia, and Serbia met for 21 days in Dayton, Ohio and agreed to the creation of a single Bosnian state composed of Serb and Bosniak-Croat entities. Unfortunately, relationships in the region remain unstable.

36. B: The Supreme Court decided the case of *Montejo v. Louisiana* in 2009; therefore, this case represents the only listed decision to occur after the Cold War ended in 1991. In this case, the Supreme Court ruled that a defendant might waive the right to counsel for police interrogation, even if that interrogation was initiated after the defendant asserted that right at an arraignment or other proceeding. This decision overruled the ruling in *Michigan v. Jackson* (1986). The decision in *Gideon v. Wainwright* (A) was made in 1963, and ruled that any person charged with a serious criminal offense had the right to an attorney and to be provided one if they could not afford it. The 1964 decision in *Escobedo v. Illinois* (C) ruled that a person in police custody had the right to consult an attorney. The 1966 decision in *Miranda v. Arizona* (D) ruled that police must inform suspects of their rights to remain silent, to have a lawyer, to be appointed a lawyer if they cannot afford one, and for interrogation to stop if they invoke their right to remain silent. After this case, these rights have been commonly referred to as "Miranda rights," and arrests or interrogations wherein police do not "Mirandize" or inform suspects of these rights can be thrown out for not following procedure.

37. B: Johann Gutenberg's printing press led to increased scientific knowledge and advancement as scientific texts were printed and dispersed throughout Europe. Because the distribution of such texts extended outside of Germany, options C and D may be eliminated. Gutenberg Bibles were printed using Gutenberg's press, and thus Gutenberg's invention was likely a factor in the Reformation of the Catholic Church. In fact, Martin Luther's Ninety-Five Theses (against the Catholic Church) were printed using a printing press. However, this reformation occurred alongside, rather than in place of, the advancement of scientific knowledge. This eliminates option A.

38. B: Of the cultures listed, only the Hebrews worshipped one God. Egyptians, Sumerians, Babylonians, and Hittites all practiced polytheistic religions that worshipped a host of deities.

39. C: The original six members of the European Economic Community began reducing trade barriers among its members as early as 1957. By 1992, the twelve member states were ready to further merge their national economies. The Maastricht Treaty official created the European Union and laid the groundwork for acceptance of the euro as a common currency. Member states of the UN, NATO, and OPEC share many common interests but have not attempted comparable economic integration.

40. B: The North American Free Trade Agreement (NAFTA) was established in 1994 by the United States, Canada, and Mexico in an effort to minimize trade barriers among the continent's three nations. In 2020, NAFTA was replaced by the United States–Mexico–Canada Agreement (USMCA), which expanded upon the older agreement.

41. B: Marx's focus in *The Communist Manifesto* (1848) and *Das Kapital* (1867) was on the inevitable conflict between the working class and the capitalists who own the means of production. He identified these two opposing forces as the proletariat and the bourgeoisie.

42. B: Plessy v. Ferguson (1896) found that segregated facilities for blacks and whites are not in violation of the Constitution. The doctrine of "separate but equal" was overturned in Brown v. Board of Education (1954). Marbury v. Madison (1803) established the Supreme Court's power to strike down acts of Congress that conflict with the Constitution. Gideon v. Wainwright (1963) guaranteed an attorney to anyone charged with a serious criminal offense.

43. D: According to the Tenth Amendment to the Constitution: "The powers not delegated to the United States by the Constitution, nor prohibited by it to the States, are reserved to the States respectively, or to the people." As the regulation of education and marriage are neither delegated to the federal government nor prohibited to the states, they are powers reserved for the states.

44. D: In Gibbons v. Ogden (1824), the Supreme Court concluded that the power to regulate interstate commerce was granted to Congress by the Commerce Clause of the Constitution. The decision went on to say that federal law took precedence over any contrary state laws in regard to interstate trade. Marbury v. Madison (1803) addressed the issue of judicial review. Dartmouth College v. Woodward (1819) held that a corporate charter is protected by the Contract Clause, which limits the state's power to affect these charters. McCulloch v. Maryland (1819) bolstered the doctrine of implied powers.

45. A: The First Amendment addresses freedom of speech, assembly, religion, and the press. A speedy trial is covered in the Sixth Amendment, cruel and unusual punishment in the Eighth Amendment, and search and seizure in the Fourth Amendment.

46. B: Charles Schenck was arrested for distributing leaflets advocating opposition to the draft during World War I. The Supreme Court unanimously decided that free speech could be restricted if it creates "a clear and present danger." This ruling was subsequently modified by Brandenburg v. Ohio in 1969. Plessy supported the "separate but equal" doctrine; Engle ruled that school prayer was unconstitutional; Miranda required police to advise criminal suspects of their rights.

47. A: A newspaper publisher in New York, Zenger, was tried for libel after publishing articles that criticized the royal governor of the state. The jury acquitted him on the grounds that he had published the truth. Freedom of the press is among the rights guaranteed by the First Amendment. The Second Amendment concerns the right to bear arms. The Third Amendment addresses the quartering of troops. The Fourth Amendment guarantees protection from unreasonable search and seizure.

48. B: Shared, or concurrent, powers are those powers held by both the states and the federal government. These include taxation, borrowing money, establishing courts, and making and enforcing laws. Implied powers are those assumed by the federal government based on the "elastic clause" in Article I of the Constitution. Expressed, or enumerated, powers are those specifically granted to the federal government in Article I, Section 8 of the Constitution—e.g., the right to coin money, declare war, and regulate interstate and foreign commerce. Reserved powers are reserved exclusively to the states.

49. A: Article I of the Constitution gives the House of Representatives the sole power of impeachment and the Senate the sole power to convict. The Chief Justice of the United States is empowered to preside over the Senate trial of a President.

50. A: Checks and balances prevent any branch of the government from running roughshod over the other two. Separation of powers refers to the distribution of specific powers among the three branches of government. Judicial review is the power of the courts to overturn legislative or executive acts that are deemed unconstitutional. Advice and consent describes the power to advise the President, ratify treaties, and confirm nominations, which is granted to the Senate in Article II of the Constitution.

51. D: The process of overriding a presidential veto is described in Article I, Section 7 of the Constitution. It requires a two-thirds vote from both the House and the Senate.

52. B: Shared, or concurrent, powers are those powers held by both the states and the federal government. While the Constitution specifically grants Congress the exclusive power to coin money, it does not specifically forbid the states from building roads, collecting taxes, and establishing courts.

53. B: The debates of 1858 resulted in Douglas's victory over Lincoln in the senatorial race. However, his performance in the debates helped make Lincoln a viable candidate for the presidency, and he was elected to that office two years later.

54. B: Article I of the Constitution mandates the taking of a census every ten years. The purpose was to be sure that each state was proportionately represented in Congress according to its population as specified in the Constitution. Census data is also used to allocate federal funding for various programs and for shaping economic policies. Individual data collected by the US Bureau of the Census is kept confidential for seventy-two years and does not affect income tax rates. Every state has two seats in the Senate regardless of population.

55. D: The Convention, organized by Lucretia Mott and Elizabeth Cady Stanton and held in upstate New York, approved a Declaration of Sentiments that proclaimed the equality of men and women. The first antislavery society in America was founded in Philadelphia in 1775. The Republican Party had its first official meeting in Jackson, Michigan in 1854. The American Temperance Society was established in Boston in 1826.

56. C: Sinclair's 1906 novel sparked public outrage by exposing the dehumanizing and unsanitary conditions prevalent in the American meatpacking industry at the turn of the century. Norris's 1901 novel depicted the conflict between wheat growers and corrupt railroad officials in California. Riis documented life in the slums of New York City in the 1880s. Steffens's muckraking journalism exposed political corruption across the country in the early years of the 20th century.

57. C: The FDIC and the SEC were both New Deal agencies created by the FDR administration in response to the stock market crash and bank failures of the Great Depression era. Both agencies still play an important role in maintaining public confidence in the nation's fundamental economic institutions.

58. D: Basing their economic principles on the biological model created by Charles Darwin, Social Darwinists advocated a laissez-faire economic policy that would allow so-called "survival of the fittest" to play out in the world of business. Their advocacy of unchecked competition was contrary to the views held by popularists, socialists, and progressives, all of whom believed that some government involvement in one form or another was essential to the functioning of a just and effective social system.

59. C: Lying at a little more than 23° south of the equator, the Tropic of Capricorn is the border between the Southern Temperate Zone to the south and the Tropical Zone to the north. The southern hemisphere is tilted toward the sun to its maximum extent each year at the winter solstice in December. The northernmost latitude at which the sun can appear directly overhead is at the Tropic of Cancer during the summer solstice. The northern and southern hemispheres are separated by the equator at 0° latitude. The eastern and western hemispheres are separated by the prime meridian at 0° longitude.

60. B: A topographic map uses contour lines to show the shape and elevation of the land. Political maps identify state and national boundaries as well as capitals and major cities. Resource maps show the natural resources and economic activities in a region. Road maps are used mainly for driving directions and trip planning.

61. B: Lines of longitude, which run north-south from pole to pole, are used to separate time zones. Houston, Texas, and Fargo, North Dakota, which are on almost the exact same line of longitude, are both in the Central Time Zone; however, they are not in the same state, do not have the same climate, and are not equidistant from the equator. To calculate distance from the equator, the latitude of the city would need to be known.

62. B: Three times the size of the continental United States, Africa contains a surprisingly small percentage of the world population. The continent is divided roughly in half by the equator. The rain forest makes up about 15 percent of central Africa.

63. C: Physical geography focuses on processes and patterns in the natural environment. What people eat in any given geographic region is largely dependent on such environmental factors as climate and the availability of arable land. Religion, family, and language may all be affected by geographical factors, but they are not as immediately affected as dietary preferences.

64. B: Overgrazing increases erosion by reducing the vegetation that naturally protects the soil from rain and wind. Rotating crops, applying mulch, and planting trees all serve to protect the soil and minimize erosion.

65. D: The taiga, or boreal forest, is found only in the North Temperate Zone between the tundra and the steppes. In addition to being the largest biome on land, it is characterized by coniferous forests and stretches across the northern regions of North America and Eurasia. Deserts, savannas, and tropical rainforests are all found at lower latitudes within the Torrid Zone.

66. D: Lying between the Tigris and Euphrates rivers, the Mesopotamian region gave rise to many prominent cultures. Today, the land belongs mainly to Iraq while extending to parts of northeastern Syria, southeastern Turkey, and southwestern Iran.

67. C: Acid rain is an example of chemical weathering. When acidic chemicals are evaporated and fall as rain, they can have devastating effects on plant and animal life. Although human activity is the primary cause of acid rain, weathering chemicals can also get into the atmosphere through oceanic bacteria and volcanoes. The other three answer choices are examples of mechanical weathering. Frost wedging occurs when water seeps into a narrow space within a rock formation and then freezes. Because water takes up more space as ice and frost than it does in its liquid state, this process can cause structural damage to the rock. Heat expansion occurs when rapid changes in temperature cause rocks to expand, leading to cracks and fissures. Salt wedging occurs when water flowing into a rock brings salt in with it. The water evaporates, but the salt is left behind, and over time the deposits of salt can create pressure within the rock.

68. B: Although both Israel and Saudi Arabia border on the Gulf of Aqaba, Jordan stands between Israel and its giant neighbor to the southeast.

69. B: Elections are not necessary to be recognized as a nation. Indeed, many nations are ruled by individuals or cabals who never allow elections to be held. Geographers assert that there are four criteria for nationhood: defined territory, government, sovereignty, and population. A nation must have land and other natural resources to exist. A nation also must have some form of government, whether it be tyrannical or democratic. Some level of central administration indicates the unity of the nation. A nation must have sovereignty; that is, it must not be directly controlled by some other country. Finally, and perhaps most obviously, a nation must have a population.

70. B: Carrie Chapman Catt (1859-1947) was serving her second term as president of the National American Woman Suffrage Association when the Nineteenth Amendment granted the vote to American women. Elected to the presidency in 1913, Wilson announced his support of women's suffrage in 1918. The National Woman's Party, which continues to function as an educational organization, was founded in 1917 to fight for the passage of a Constitutional amendment to guarantee women's suffrage. World War I ended in 1919.

71. B: As a medical student in the 1930s, Michael DeBakey (1908–2008) invented a major component of the heart-lung machine that made open-heart surgery possible. He was one of the first to perform coronary artery bypass surgery, was a pioneer in the development of an artificial heart, and performed the first successful patch-graft angioplasty. He joined the faculty of the Baylor College of Medicine in 1948 and continued to practice medicine almost until the day he died.

72. D: Opportunity cost is a measure of what a society gives up to produce a good (or goods). When the society decides to increase its production of Good X from 10 to 15 units, it gives up the ability to produce 4 units of Good Y (with production of Good Y dropping from 10 units to 6 units). The opportunity cost of the decision, then, is 4 units of Good Y.

73. D: Keynes was an influential advocate of government intervention in a domestic economy for the purpose of stimulating economic growth. Keynes believed that appropriate government action could help end a recession more quickly; such measures might involve deficit spending. Because of this, and because Keynes is not associated with the view that deficit spending leads to inflation, option A can be eliminated. Additionally, Keynes is not closely associated with advocating government action to break up monopolies; this eliminates option B. Finally, option C can be eliminated because it describes Say's Law, which is in fact the opposite of Keynes's law: demand creates its own supply.

74. B: Unemployment leads to lost productivity because people who would be productive if employed (thus contributing to economic growth) are not economically productive when they do not have work. Option A can be rejected because high unemployment is not typically thought to be a central cause of inflation; rather, high levels of unemployment might instead contribute to deflation (an overall decrease in prices). Option C can be rejected because unemployment would tend to have the effect of decreasing aggregate demand rather than increasing it, simply because fewer people would have money with which to make purchases. Option D can be rejected because unemployment is less likely to increase aggregate supply than to reduce it (fewer people working means fewer people producing goods and services).

75. C: Economists are interested in unemployment caused by changes in the business cycle. That is what cyclical unemployment measures. There will always be some measure of structural and frictional unemployment, and those are not typically considered when assessing the unemployment picture in a nation.

76. D: When there is a lot of unemployment, the AS curve is horizontal. If AD decreases at this time, prices will tend to remain the same while GDP decreases. When there is full employment, the AS curve is vertical. If AD decreases at this time, prices will drop but GDP will tend to remain the same.

77. C: The graph shows a shift in demand, with a corresponding increase in the price of SuperCell Batteries. The shift is illustrated by the two demand curves, with Demand 2 curve illustrating an increase in price. Because the price has increased, not decreased, this eliminates option A. The equilibrium point is the point at which the quantity demanded equals the quantity supplied. The graph shows two equilibrium points, the first where Demand 1 meets the supply curve, and the second where Demand 2 meets the supply curve. Because equilibrium has shifted, option B can be eliminated. Regarding option D, a double coincidence of wants occurs when two people each have a good or service the other wants, giving rise to the possibility of trade (without money). The graph does not illustrate anything regarding a double coincidence of wants, so option D can be rejected on that basis.

78. B: As a strict constructionist, Jefferson argued that the Constitution did not make any provision for the creation of a federal bank. Jefferson was a leader of the Democratic-Republicans who opposed the establishment of a powerful central government. He believed that the Bank would give an unfair advantage to the more industrial northern states.

79. B: Lower interest rates allow banks to lend out more money, which serves to stimulate consumer spending. Increased spending tends to raise, not lower, prices. The Federal Reserve

Board is not actively involved in international trade. The fear of inflation usually leads to a rise in interest rates.

80. C: Formulated in the early 19th century, Malthus's theory that population increase would ultimately outpace increases in the means of subsistence did not anticipate technological advances in food production and birth control; nevertheless, the theory was highly influential in the formulation of subsequent economic and social policies.

81. A: Converting nominal GDP to real GDP requires some measure of the change in prices of goods and services within a nation over time. One could use the Consumer Price Index—the value of a fixed "market basket" of goods and services on a yearly basis—to determine the rate of inflation and then adjust nominal GDP to real GDP.

82. D: None of the options listed are true. Excess reserves will increase by $80,000, as the bank must keep 20% of the deposit, or $20,000, leaving $80,000. The money multiplier is one divided by the reserve ratio, or 5 $\left(1 \div \frac{1}{5} = 5\right)$. This means the money supply could increase a total of $500,000 $(\$100{,}000 + (5 \times \$80{,}000) = \$500{,}000)$.

83. C: Brazil is the 10th largest producer of oil in the world and the largest in South America. Venezuela is the second largest producer of oil in South America and has the world's largest oil reserves. Bolivia and Guatemala produce oil but are not major producers in Latin America. Uruguay has no significant petroleum production.

84. B: If interest rates in the US increase, foreign investors may send more money to the US. Those investors would have to first exchange their currencies for American dollars, making the American dollars more valued (scarce) and therefore increase in value.

85. D: Anthropology is the study of human social relationships and the analysis of cultural characteristics. Economists study how societies use resources and distribute goods. Political science is the study of government and political institutions. Psychologists focus on mental functions and human behavior.

86. C: Johnson exerted his presidential power to advance the Great Society agenda and to enact major civil rights legislation. He also conducted a war in Vietnam without Congressional declaration. Jefferson, Hoover, and Reagan were all outspoken advocates of limiting the role of government, including the executive branch.

87. B: Middle-grade students should be expected to transfer information from one medium to another, including written to visual and statistical to written or visual, while using computer software as appropriate. The other choices represent important skills that are less directly relevant to the student's ability to communicate ideas in various forms.

88. D: While all social science is concerned to some extent with how societies make use of whatever resources are available to them, the production and distribution of goods is of primary concern to the economist.

89. A: A primary source is a document or object that was created at the time of an event. Primary sources include such things as original manuscripts, letters, official records, and photographs. Secondary sources, such as textbooks and encyclopedia articles, are removed by one or more steps from the original event. They offer interpretation or analysis based on primary sources.

90. C: Paleoanthropologists combine the disciplines of paleontology and physical anthropology to study ancient humans. Archaeology is the systematic study of past cultures by the recovery of artifacts and other material evidence. Excavating the Olduvai Gorge in eastern Africa, Leakey (1903-1972) and his team confirmed the theory that human life originated in that region. Leakey's primary interest was not the analysis of economic, social, and political systems, nor was he actively searching for animal bones.